CARVING CARICATURE FIGURES

FROM SCRATCH

W. "Pete" LeClair

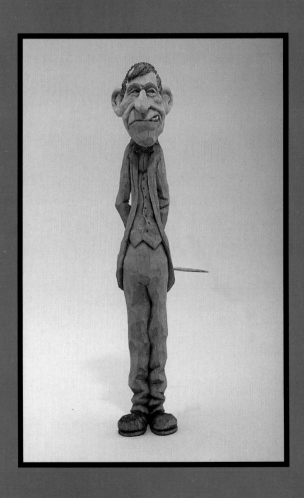

Schiffer Publishing Ltd ®

4880 Lower Valley Road, Atglen, PA 19310 USA

Published by Schiffer Publishing Ltd.
4880 Lower Valley Road
Atglen, PA 19310
Phone: (610) 593-1777; Fax: (610) 593-2002
E-mail: Schifferbk@aol.com
Please visit our web site catalog at
www.schifferbooks.com
We are always looking for people to write books on new
and related subjects. If you have an idea for a book
please contact us at the above address.

This book may be purchased from the publisher.
Include $3.95 for shipping.
Please try your bookstore first.
You may write for a free catalog.

In Europe, Schiffer books are distributed by
Bushwood Books
6 Marksbury Ave.
Kew Gardens
Surrey TW9 4JF England
Phone: 44 (0) 20 8392-8585; Fax: 44 (0) 20 8392-9876
E-mail: Bushwd@aol.com
Free postage in the U.K., Europe; air mail at cost.

Copyright © 2001 by Pete LeClair
Library of Congress Card Number: 00-106245

Designed by John P. Cheek
Type set in Lydian BT/Korinna

ISBN: 0-7643-1233-2
Printed in China

Contents

Introduction

Since I wrote my first book, *Carving Caricature Heads & Faces*, a lot has happened. I retired from the job I had had for over twenty years, moved to a smaller house, and began carving and teaching full-time. My carving has taken me across the country and around the world...at least all the way to Australia. It has been fun!

This book focuses on carving a whole figure caricature from scratch. Of course I still find that most of the personality of the character I am carving comes through the face, but the body adds to the overall effect and makes the figure come to life. This book starts with a simple block of bass wood, and goes all the way through carving and painting of a figure.

The methods are similar to the first book, though I have learned a few new tricks in the years since then. I still strive to get proportions correct, even if the features are exaggerated. If that doesn't happen the figure is not believable. The humorous additions follow the basic carving techniques. All in all, I hope that the method I am sharing will help you move step-by-step toward a successful caricature figure.

One important note! You will notice in some of the picture that the thumb of my knife hand has a pretty heavy coating of tape on it. This too is something new since my last book. While I always wore a protective glove on my holding hand, I only wore a light cotton covering on the thumb of my knife hand. I thought nothing of the little nicks that the knife would make in my thumb as I carved. Then a couple of years ago one of these nicks became severely infected, to the point where it spread beyond the thumb and actually became life-threatening. Now I tape several layers of masking tape over the thumb. This keeps the knife from going through to the skin. If it starts to get a little ratty, I just add another layer or two.

Anyway, I wish you safe and happy carving as you create these delightful caricatures.

Carving

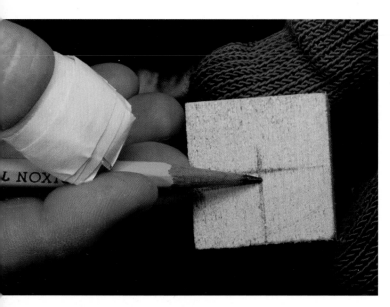

I begin on the head area before turning to the body. I want to block out the head, and I start by quartering the end of the block.

The length of the neckline determines whether the face will be longer or shorter. The longer the neckline the longer the face, the shorter the neckline the shorter the face. With a finger against the top, draw the line at the back of the neck.

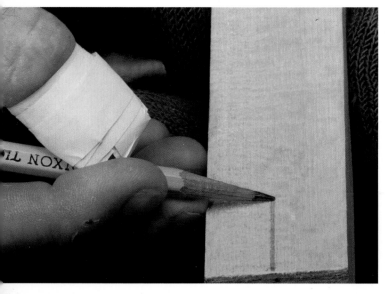

Continue all the way around the block.

On one side draw a profile line from the back neckline at an angle down to where the front neckline will be.

Carry the line across the front of the neck...

Using your finger as a stop, transfer the line to the other side.

then join the back and front necklines with another diagonal line on the other side.

Draw the line for the back of the ear. The placement is your call...

Caricature carvers can cheat a little, so one of "Pete's Rules" is to put the ears a little further back than the art books say. I draw the line for the front of the ears slightly behind the center mark.

but be sure the other side is the same.

Mark the top of the ear on both sides.

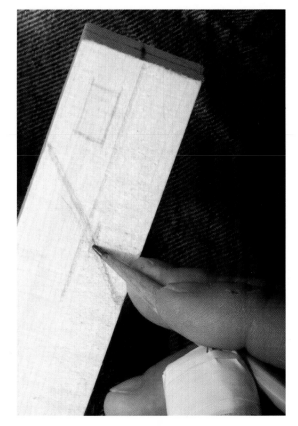

Do the same on the other side.

Do the same with the bottoms of the ears, marking both sides to be the same.

Slightly in front of the centerline, mark the front of the neck at the collar.

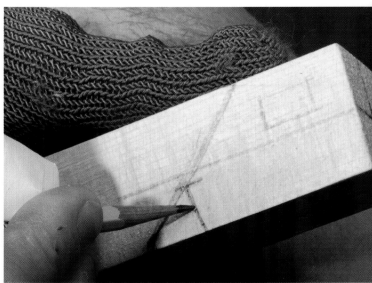

From that mark, draw the chin line. This can be any angle, as long as both sides match.

To insure this draw the chin line across the front of the face...

For safety I always slice in toward the center of the wood. Start with the tip...

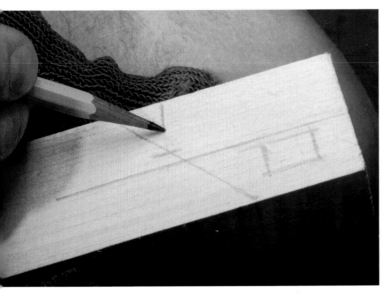

and back to the neck mark on the other side.

and push in toward the center.

The head markings complete.

This way the knife stays in the wood and doesn't pop out to cut the carver. This first cut is on the front corner, starting at the collar line and cutting up toward the chin.

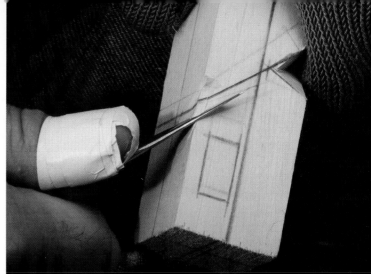

This will take a couple of cuts. Clean out the first cut by cutting back to it from below the chin line.

Notch out the back corners of the neck.

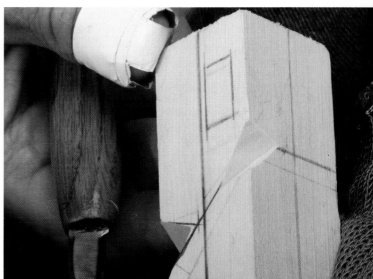

Go back and deepen the cut, using the same cut method.

Progress. Repeat on the other two corners.

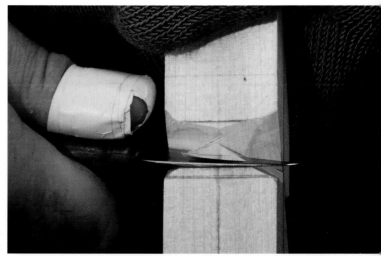

One corner complete. I repeat this at all four corners.

Now I can work on the center of the four sides. We have already removed a lot of wood, making the center work much easier. I start on the front to define the chin. This is the same back and forth notching I used on the corners.

Continue until you have a well-defined chin.

Mark the front corners of the head for removal. This is probably the most important step. This makes all the difference between a realistic looking face and a blocky face.

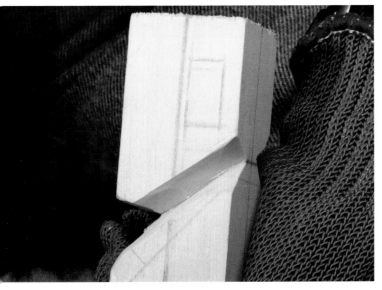

Continue up both sides...

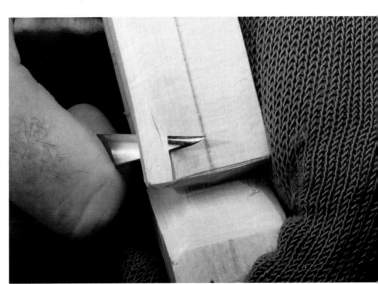

Simply knock the front corners off.

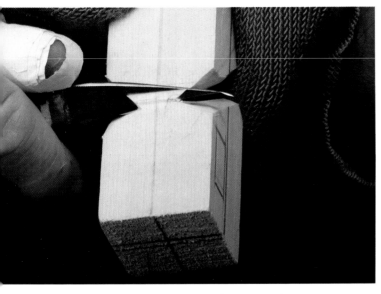

and finally the back. The back doesn't need much carving.

Do both sides.

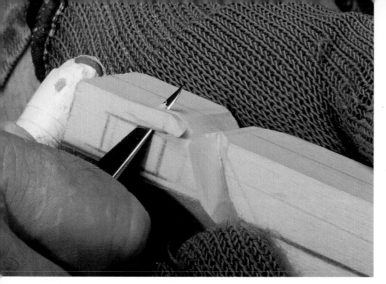

Following the line of the back of the ear, knock of the back corners of the head at a 45 degree angle.

Draw a second line from the tip of the nose to the front of the chin.

Do the same on the other side for this result.

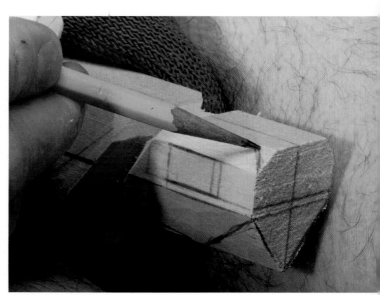

At the back of the head mark the corner for removal. Copy the marks to the other side of the head.

Draw a line from the tip of the nose up to top of the head to create a profile. The exact positions are up to you and will determine the character of the carving.

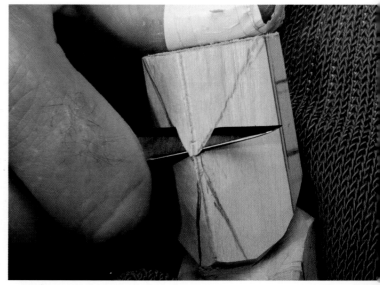

Knock off the areas marked, above the nose..

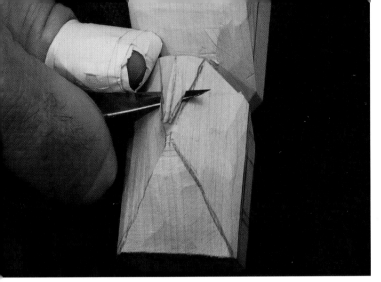

and below...

Remove the area above the ears with a scooping cut starting at the top line of the ear. The depth of the cut is up to the carver.

for this result.

Since this is a thin face, I will continue with the scooping cut until I am halfway to the center line. Do the other side in the same way.

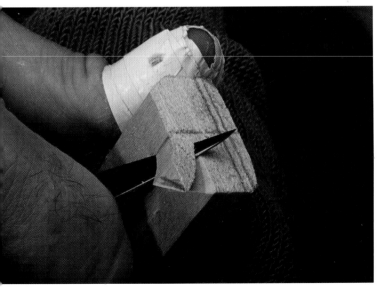

Cut off the top edge of the back of the head.

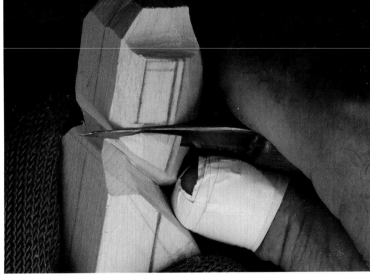

Use the same scooping cut under the ears, starting at the bottom line. Do both sides.

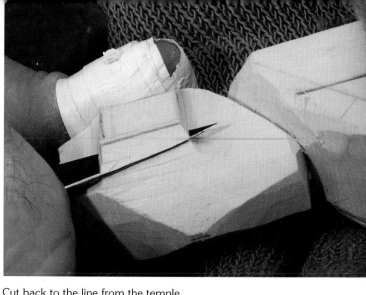

Cut back to the line from the temple.

Progress.

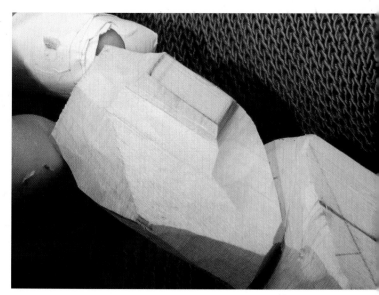

The result.

Next we block out the ears. Start by gently rocking the blade into the front line of the ear, using light, steady pressure to get to the depth I need.

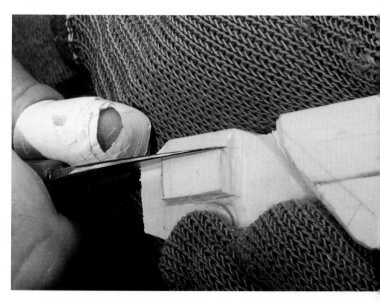

Do the same thing at the back of the ear.

Do the other side of the ear for this result.

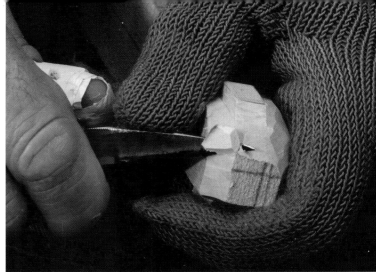

and around the back.

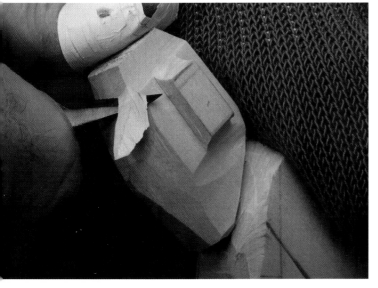

Shape the head to remove all the flat areas. I start on the forehead ridge...

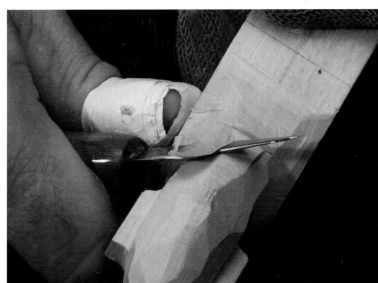

The same process continues down the lower face.

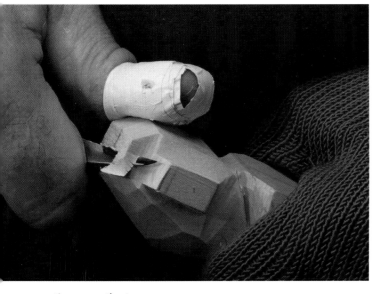

continue over the top...

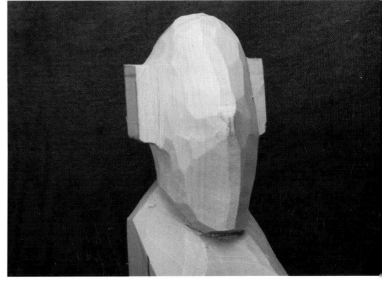

When all the flat surfaces are rounded we are ready to define facial features.

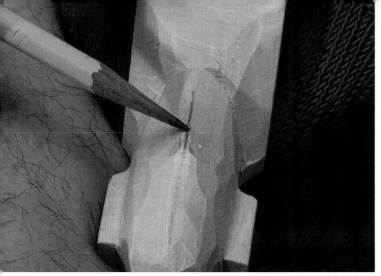

Redraw the centerline.

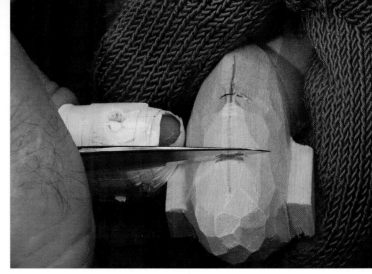

Make a stop cut into the line of the bridge of the nose...

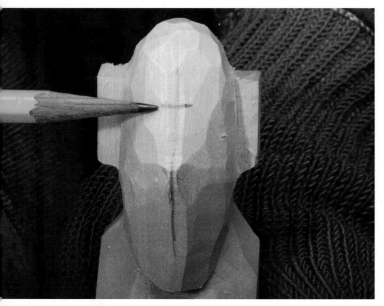

Slightly below the top of the ears, mark the bridge of the nose.

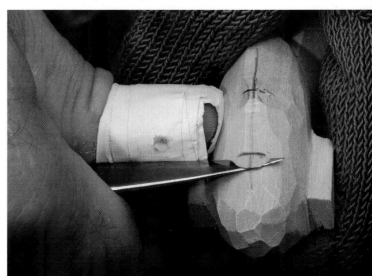

and cut back to it from the forehead.

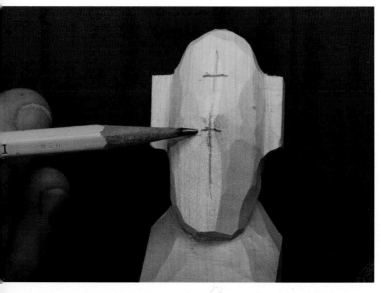

Slightly above the bottom of the ears, mark the end of the nose.

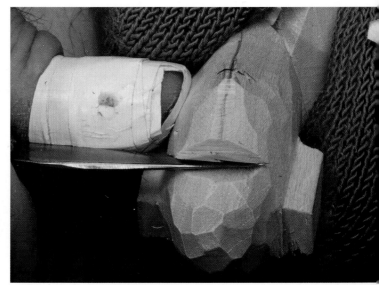

Deepen the cut by repeating the process.

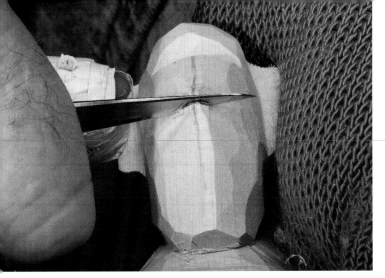

Repeat the process under the nose. Make a stop cut in...

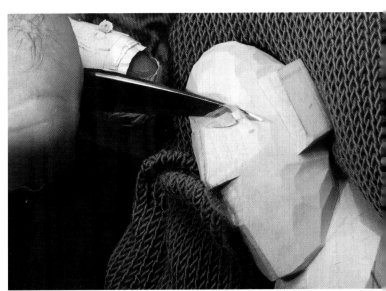

The corner of the eye is at a slightly downward angle from the bridge. Cut a stop into this line...

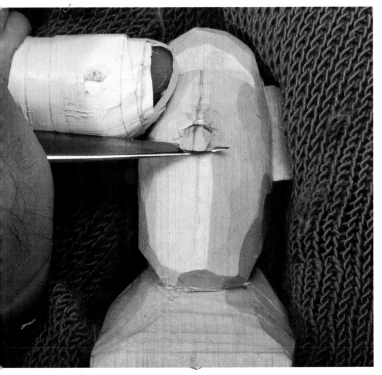

and cut back to it from the lip. This cut is with the grain, so go very easy. If you don't it is very easy to cut off the nose

Progress from the side...

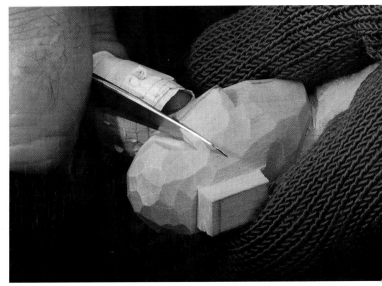

and trim back to it from the forehead.

Do the same on the other side, being sure to match the angles.

Where the nose and eye area meet I switch to an #11 gouge (3mm), because the knife does not get into this space well.

Next I am going to scoop out these areas beside the nose.

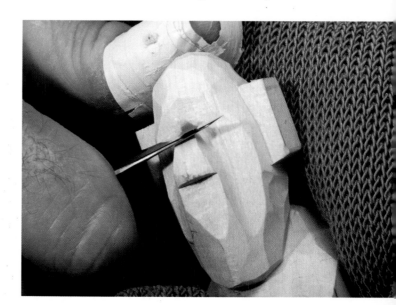

Shape the front of the nose.

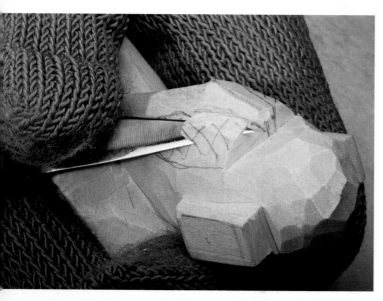

This is done with the knife, using a slicing cut.

Progress from the front...

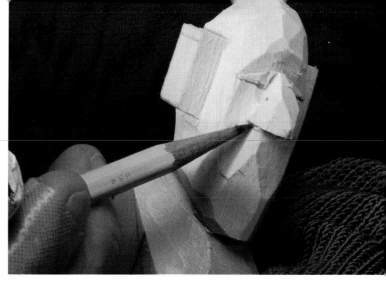

Draw the line of the bottom of the nose going into the face.

and the side.

This is the point where I determine the expression of the character. If his mouth is to be cocked to one side, I can adjust other facial features to make that look natural. I am going to make this fellow with a big toothy grin on the left of his face. I start by bring an expression line down from the right corner of the nose.

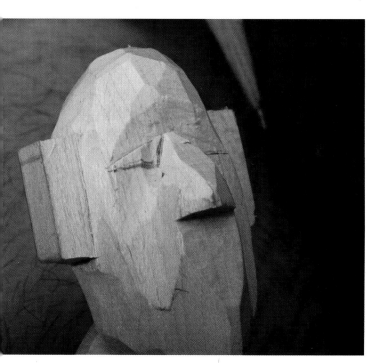

A line from the outer corner to the nose defines the lower eyelid. Draw it in on both sides.

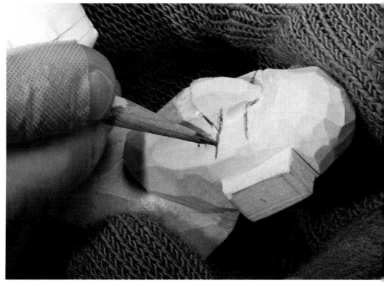

On the other side, where the smile will be, the expression line goes out much more flatly.

You can see the difference here.

Lay the knife against the forehead area and slice down to the lower lid.

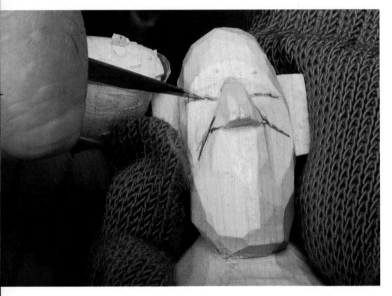

Now that the expression is set, I can carve the eyes. Using the tip of the knife I follow the bottom lid line with three light cuts (as opposed to one deep cut), because we are going across the grain.

Next make a deep cut beside the nose so we can relieve the wood.

The result.

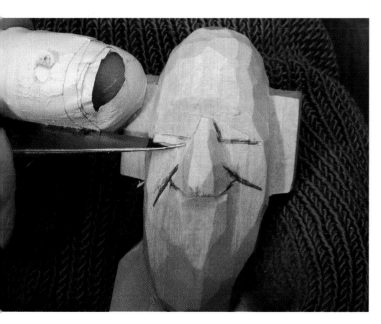

Bevel off the lower lid ridge. Repeat the process on the other eye. The expression comes in the top of the eye, so the lower lids are basically the same, just as you drew them earlier.

Make a stop cut on the expression line.

Remove the wood on the upper lip between the expression line and the bottom of the nose.

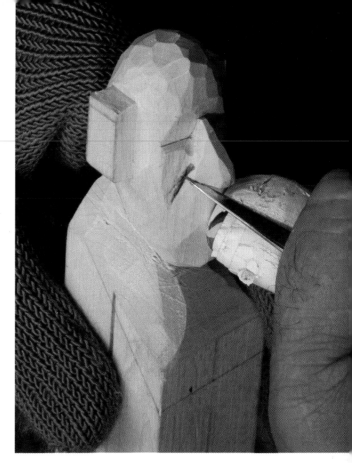

Next make a stop cut on the bottom of the nose back to the expression line.

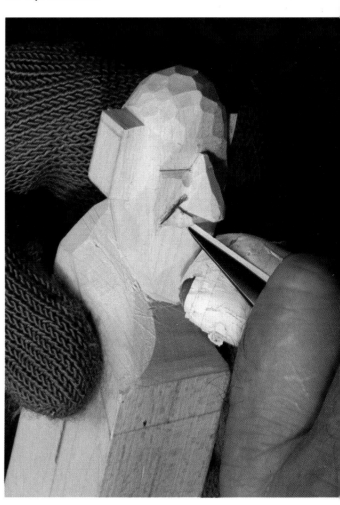

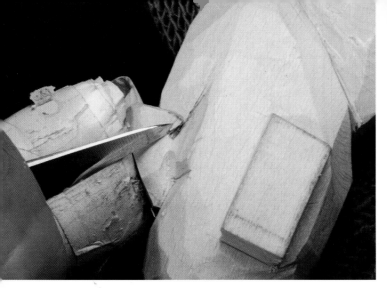

Cut a small wedge out at the back of nostril, going back to the face.

Draw in the shape of the ears...

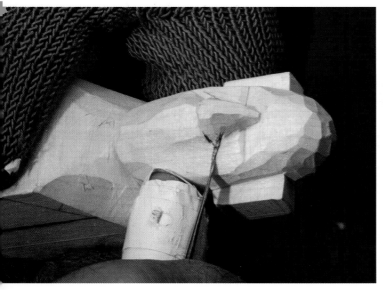

Follow the same steps on the other side.

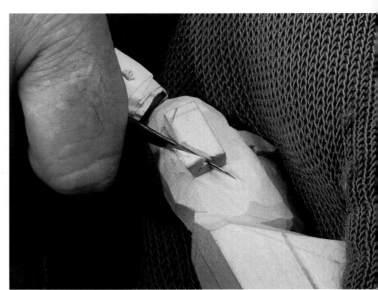

and cut into the lines with a straight cut.

The result. Remember the asymmetry.

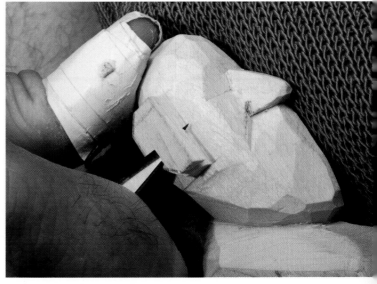

Bevel the surface of the ears.

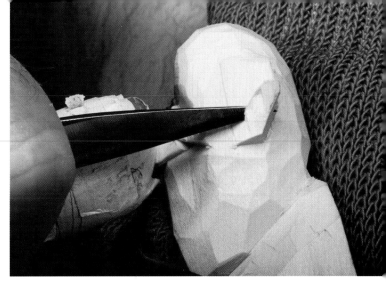

Make a scoop cut on the back lower edge.

The result.

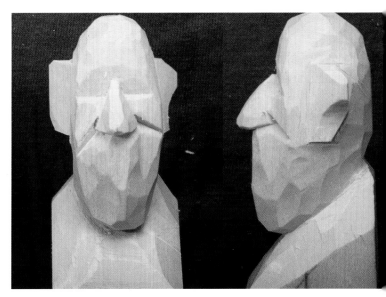

The result can be seen on his left ear.

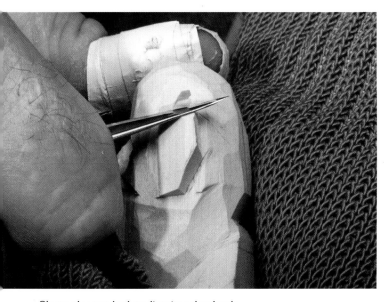

Shape the top by beveling its edge back.

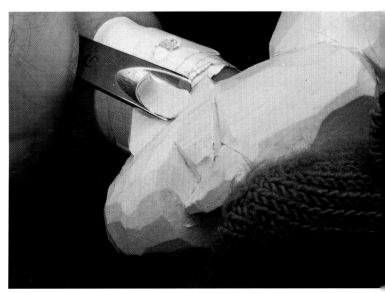

Use a gouge to hollow out the ear. I start in the middle and come at an angle toward the front.

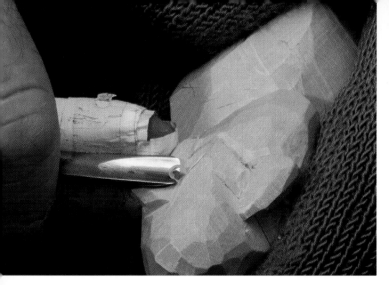

Then I start at the back and follow the upper curve of the ear around to the front.

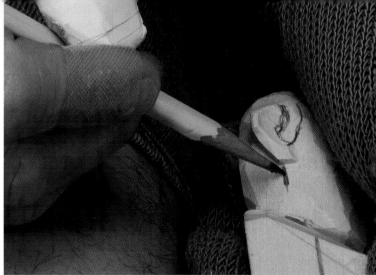

Draw in the jaw line. First come down from the ear...

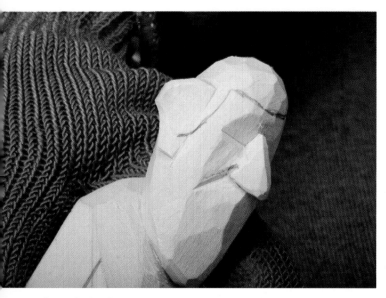

Draw the hairline carrying the sideburn into the ear.

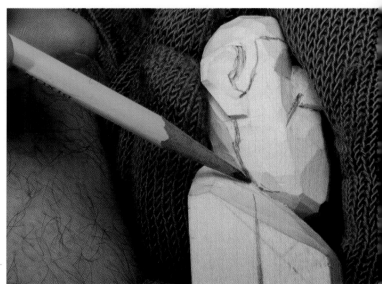

then turn the line forward. Many beginning carvers forget to bring the line down, coming forward from the ear lobe instead of below it.

The back of the sideburn also curves back toward the ear.

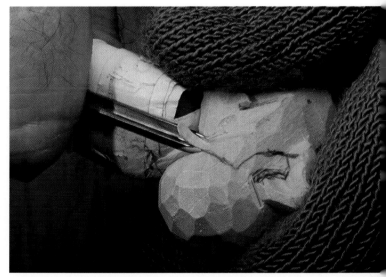

I use a #11 (3mm) gouge to cut in the hairline and the jaw line. Cutting in the hairline gives the face the thinness it needs. I like to start at the center of the forehead and work to the outside.

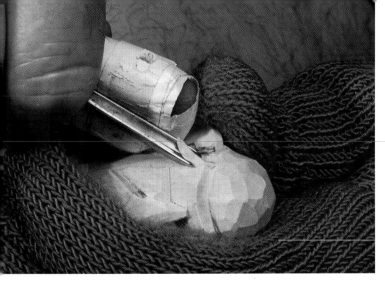

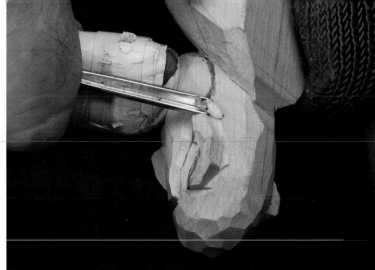

Next I work up from the cheekbone. This is a deeper line and I go over it twice. This brings in the temple area so it is deeper than the cheek area, popping out the cheeks.

around the earlobe...

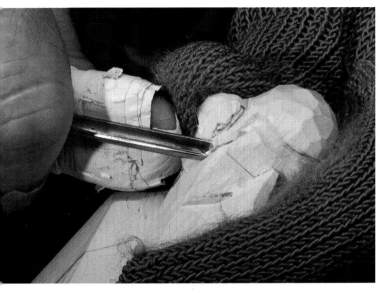

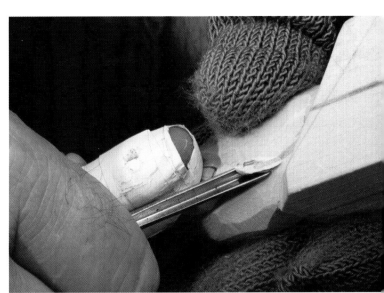

and down the jaw line. Do the other side the same way.

Gouge from the end of the sideburn back to the cheekbone.

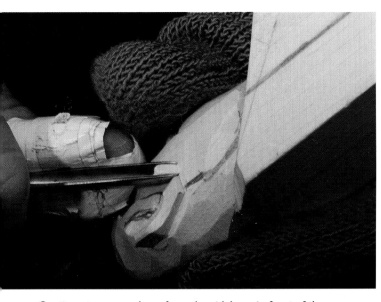

Continue to gouge down from the sideburn in front of the ear...

The result.

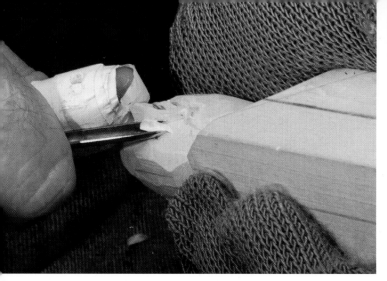

Cutting into the hair behind the ear (not undercutting the ear), follow the line of ear back to join the previous cut.

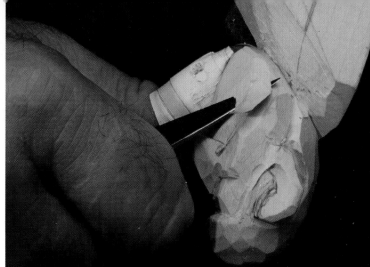

Now we can begin to add the exaggeration. I trim off the bottom jaw on the right side of the face to give movement to the mouth on the left.

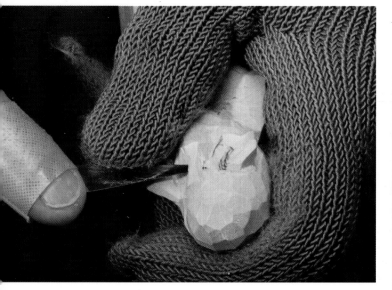

Blend the face into the gouge marks you have just made. This will thin the face, giving us the gaunt look we are seeking.

Remove enough of the face to get rid of the ridge the gouge made. Go all around the head.

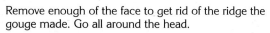

Progress.

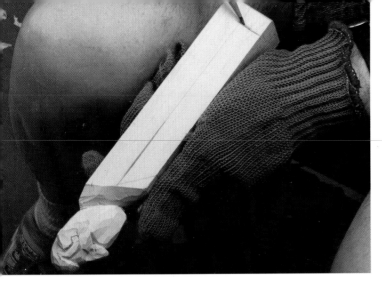

On one side draw in the top of the shoe...

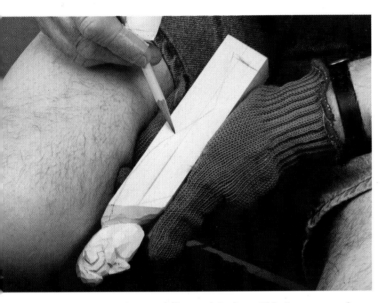

and the spine and general shape of the legs. This line more or less represents the bone line.

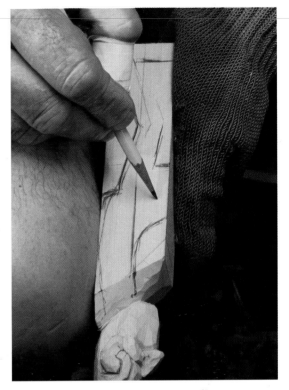

It's a little early to draw in the hands, but I need to leave plenty of wood.

Now draw in details like the rump and the back of the legs.

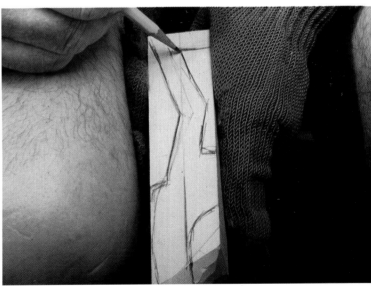

Continue drawing the front of the leg.

then the middle.

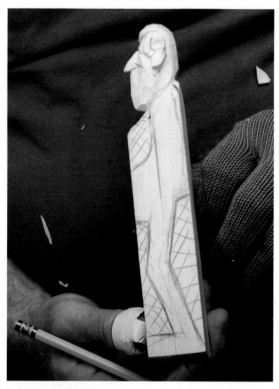

The next task is to remove the excess material as marked here.

Below the hands make a stop cut...

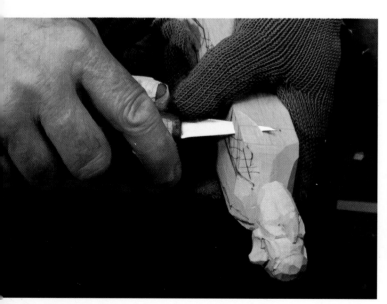

Do both corners...

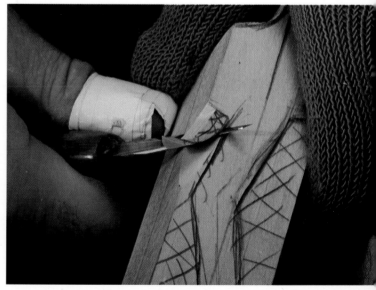

and cut back to it. Do the same thing at the top of the shoes.

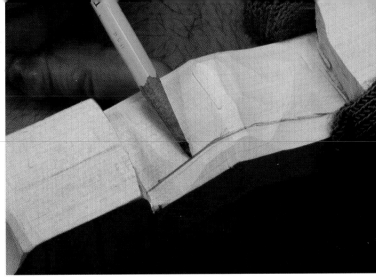

The outside leg will be carved away from the hand to the foot. Mark it for removal.

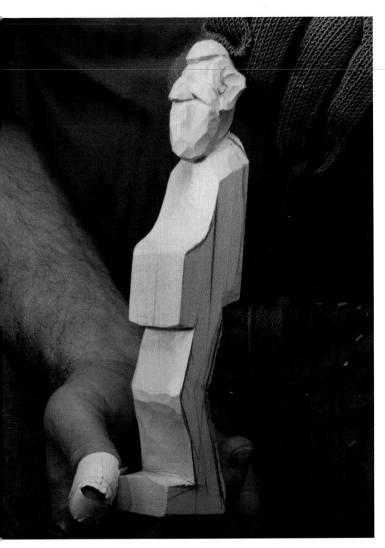

Progress.

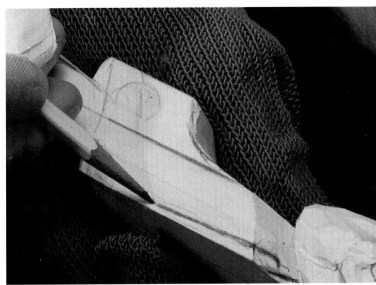

The left arm will bent. Draw a reference line (the basic bone line) of the upper arm to the elbow...

Determine where the right arm will go and mark it.

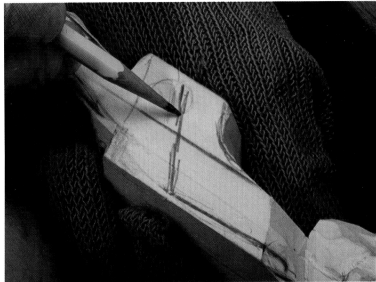

and from the elbow to the hand.

Draw in the slight bend in the reference line for the right arm.

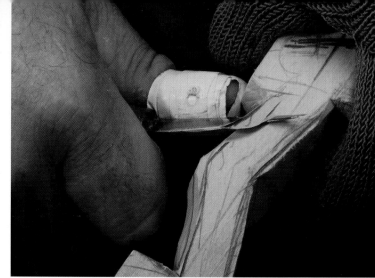

and carve the leg back to it.

Draw the outside of the leg under the left arm.

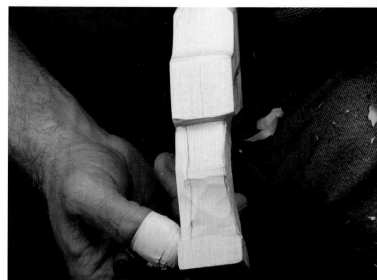

Continue to trim to this point, then do the other side.

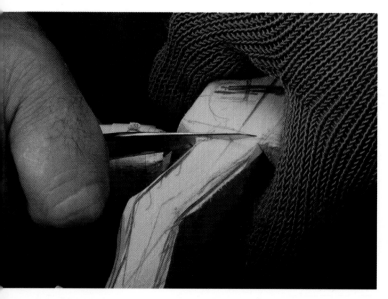

At the top corner of the left leg make a stop cut...

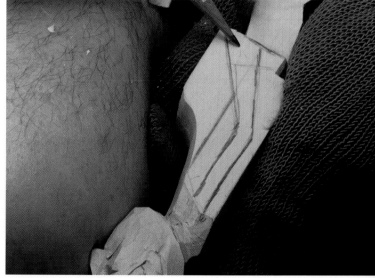

Draw out the right arm. I don't draw in the hand yet, but do flare the drawing out to leave lots of room for it.

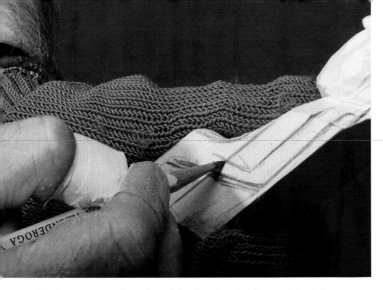

Do the same on the other side, drawing the front of the left arm...

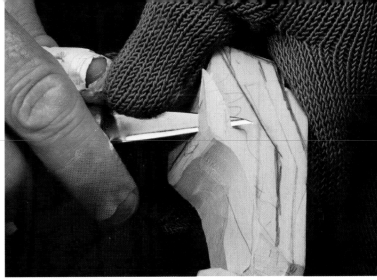

Remove the wood, starting with the corners. Most of this is done with the knife.

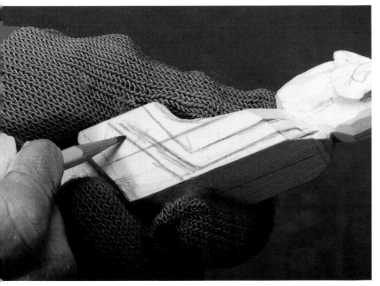

and the back.

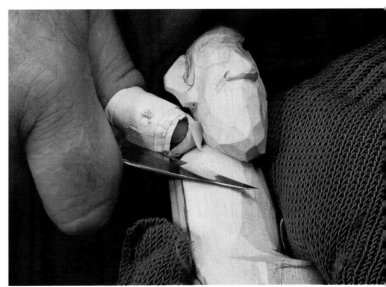

Round over the chest area.

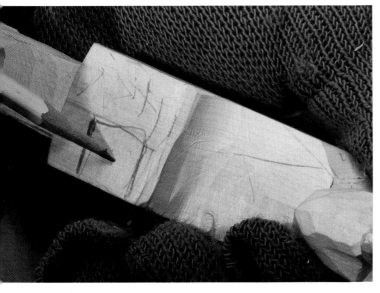

This is the block for the left hand. All the material around it, back to the front surfaces of the arms will be removed, leaving the rounded chest.

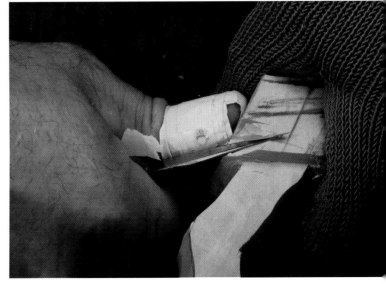

Continue the wood removal under the arm.

Use a wide gouge to block out the hand. A knife in here would chew up the wood more than I like.

Progress.

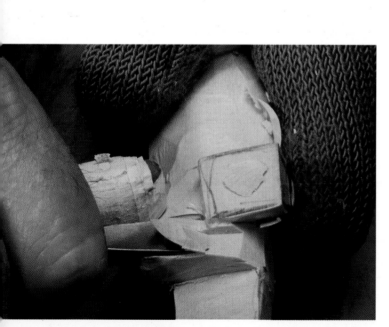

Use a flat gouge to clean up the carving.

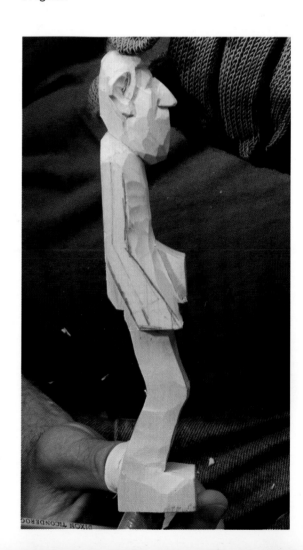

30

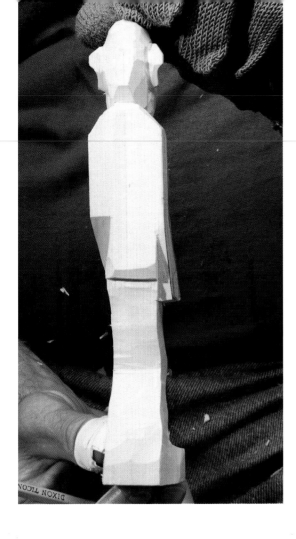

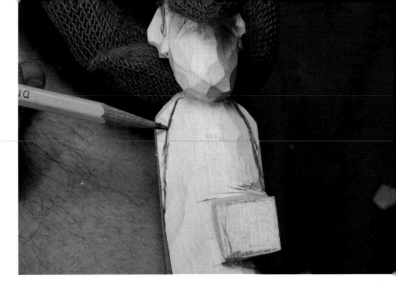

Draw in the line of the shoulders...

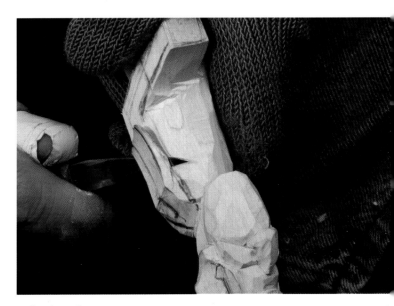

and reduce them.

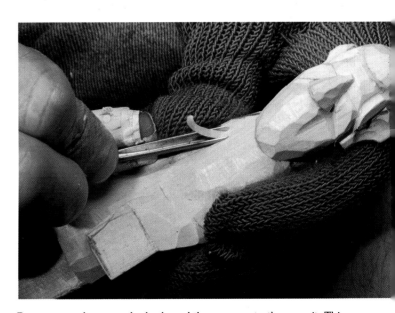

Run a gouge between the body and the arm, up to the armpit. This defines the body and give thickness to the arm.

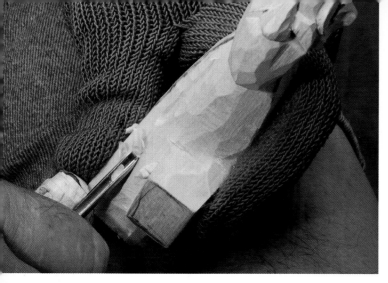

Do the same with the lower arm...

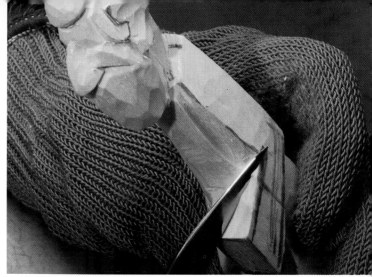

I am going to cut of this corner of the lower arm...

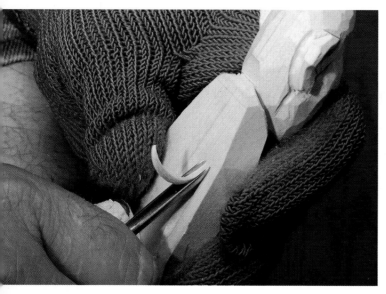

and the back.

for this result.

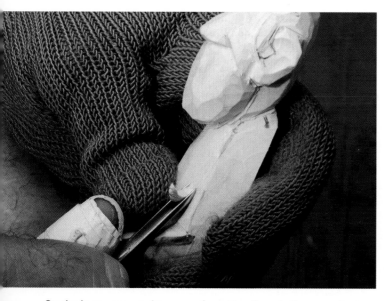

On the bent arm run the gouge from the elbow to the arm pit.

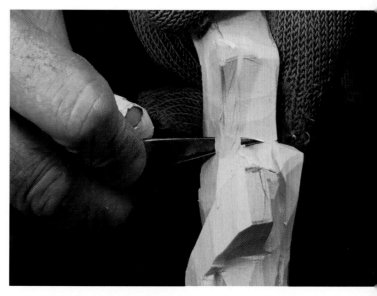

Knock off all the 90 degree edges on the body. This is done basically with a 45 degree cut which will be rounded later.

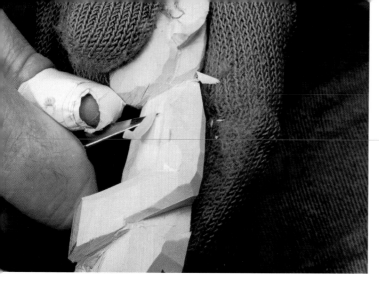

Round the body over into the gouge line, removing the gouge ridge in the process.

Use a smaller gouge to outline the shirt line, front and back.

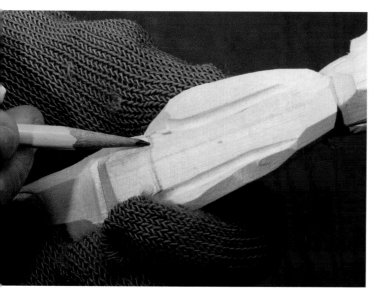

Draw in the shirt line, starting in the back and carrying the line around to the front. I will remove some of the wood in the area of the pants to bring out the shirt.

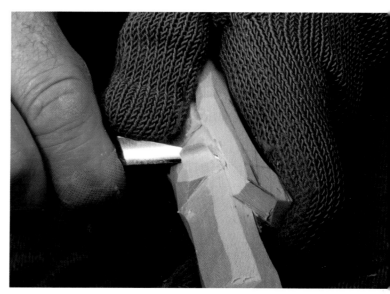

Shape the pants.

Use a gouge to get in this area of the pants in the front.

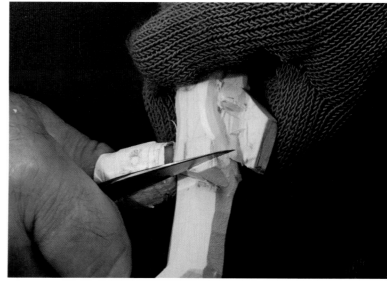

The right hand is in an open fist. The bottom angles slightly upward toward the front. Make a stop cut in this line and...

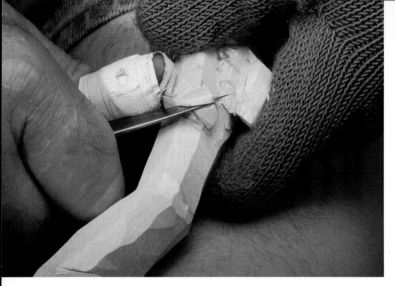

and cut back to it, reducing the area to the level of the pants leg.

This takes the arm to roughly the size and shape we want. Repeat on the other arm.

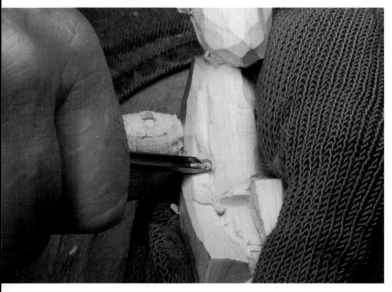

Use a gouge to create the crook in the arm at the elbow.

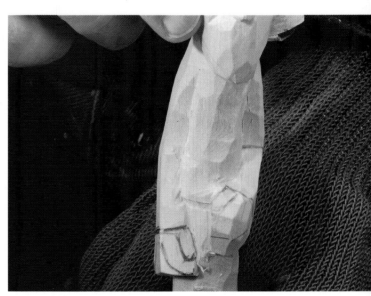

Draw in the top view of the hands. The lower hand is an open fist, and the top hand is closed. This drawing will set the planes that are carved next.

Begin to thin and shape the arm using a wide gouge. A knife in here has a tendency to score the carving.

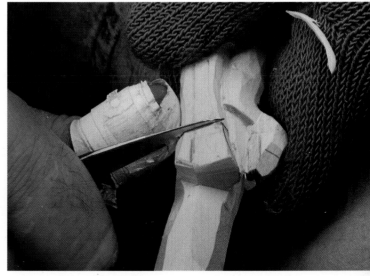

Make a stop cut in the cuffs.

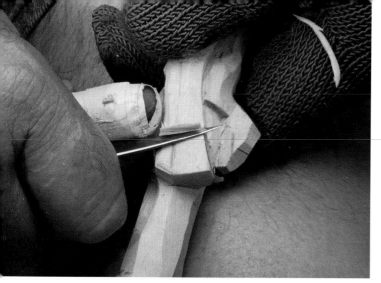

Carve back to it from the hand, going all around it.

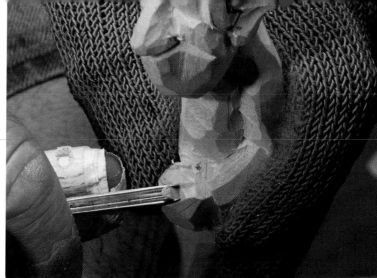

With a number 11 gouge, run up the finger next to the thumb on both sides.

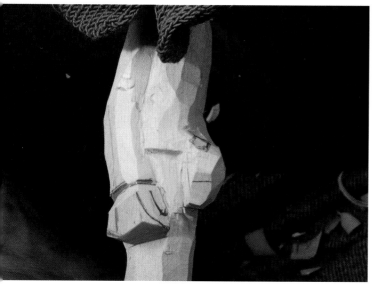

Progress. Do the same on the other hand.

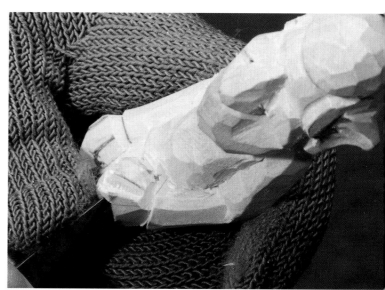

With a knife take off the ridge the gouge left, lowering the finger.

Shape the planes of the hands.

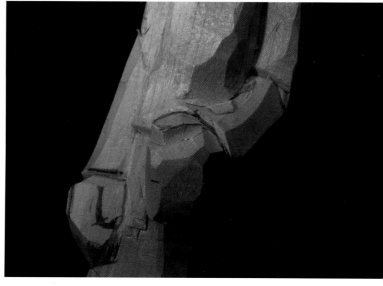

The left hand blocked out. Do the same on the right hand.

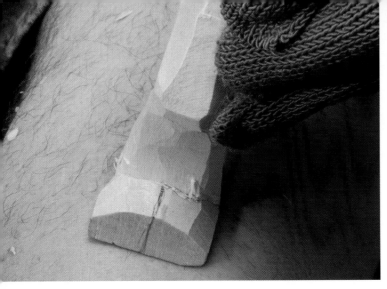

Draw the center line of the feet.

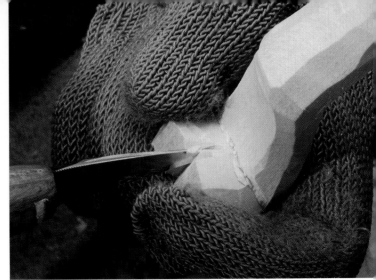

On the top of the shoes, carry the V back to the pants.

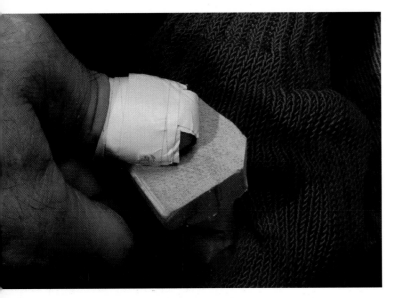

Knock off the outside corners of the feet.

The body is blocked out.

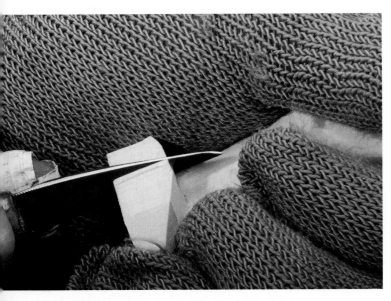

Cut a V out of the center to separate the shoes.

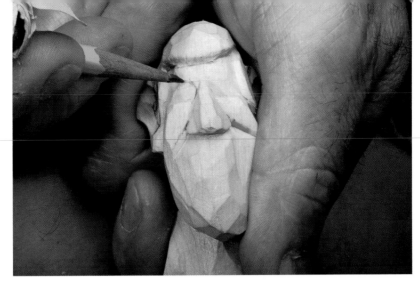

Starting at the inside corner of the eye draw the line of the eye socket, arching it higher than the bridge of the nose on the right eye—the normal eye.

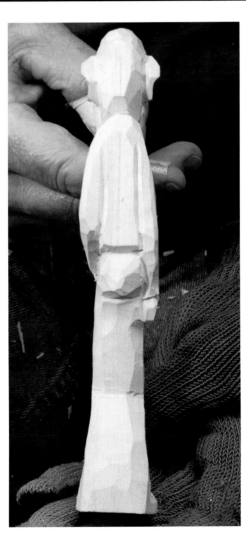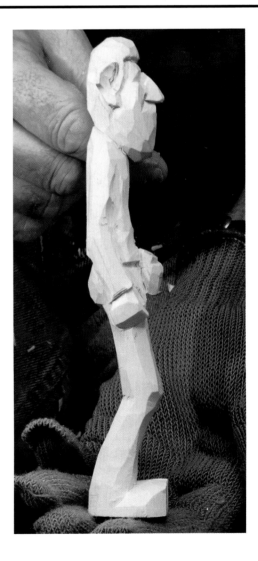

Continue the line down to a point below the lower eyelid.

and the lower line, not quite as low.

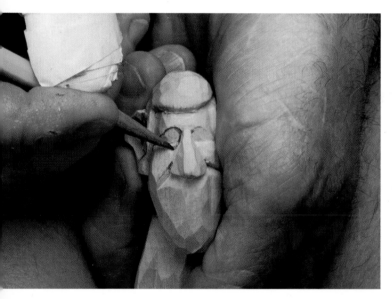

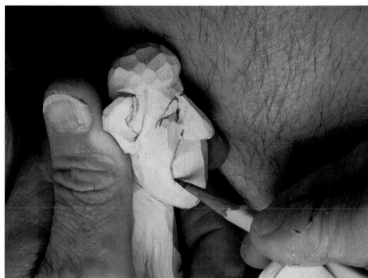

Return to inside corner and draw the line of the bag below the eye.

Extend the expression lines.

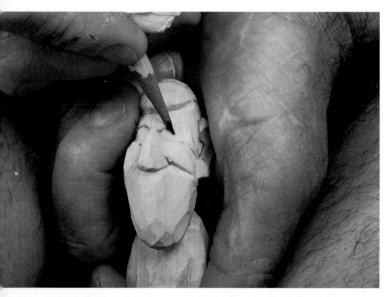

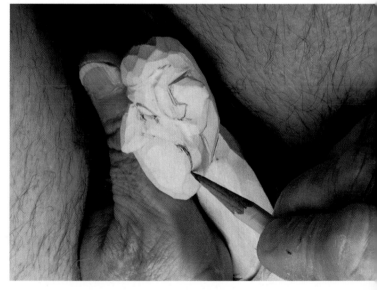

The left eye is done the same way, but because the smile is going to be on this side of the face, the eye will squint. Draw the upper line not quite as high...

Again, on the smiley side of the face the line will extend out further before it drops down.

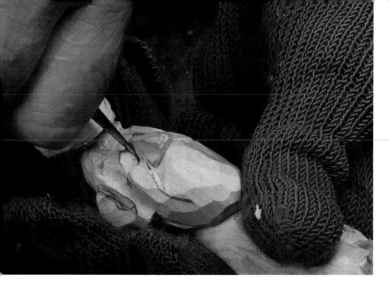

Cut a stop in the line of the eye, starting beside the nose...

Starting at the same point, carve down the line you drew for the bag under the eye. Go only to the end of the line you drew. Repeat on the other eye.

over the top...

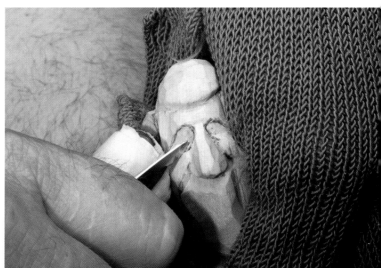

Cut a wedge on the inside of the eye socket back to the nose. This gives curvature to the eye socket.

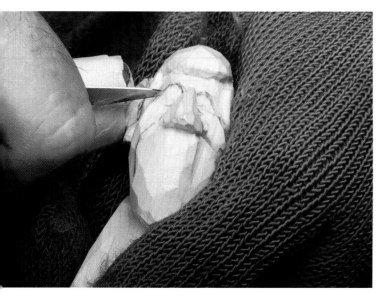

and out to the end. Some of this cut will be across the grain and should be done with repeated light strokes. Repeat on the other eye.

The result. Do the same on the other eye.

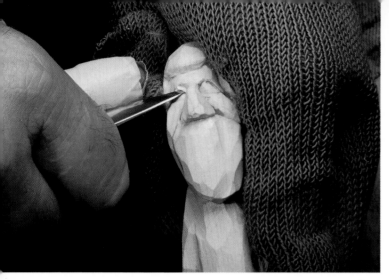

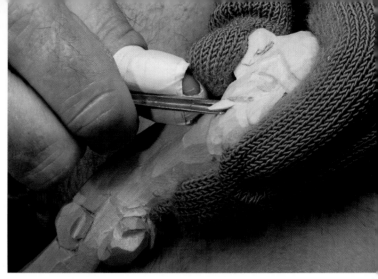

Three more small wedges are needed to shape the eye socket. They follow the arching stop you just cut at the top of the eye. The first goes up toward the top of the arch.

With a gouge follow the expression lines, being sure to take the wood off the lip side of the line.

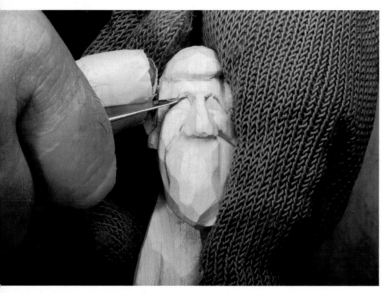

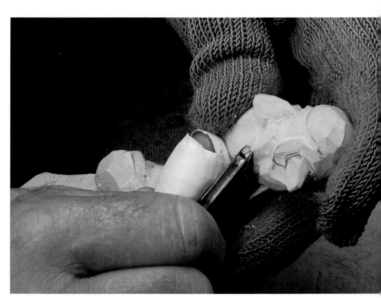

The second goes across the top.

On the exaggerated line the grain direction changes so I need to cut in two directions. Up first...

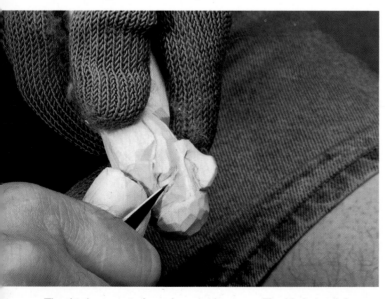

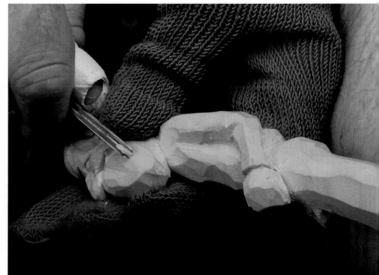

The third comes in from the outside corner. The blade in all three should be flat against the eye socket mound. Repeat on the other eye.

then down.

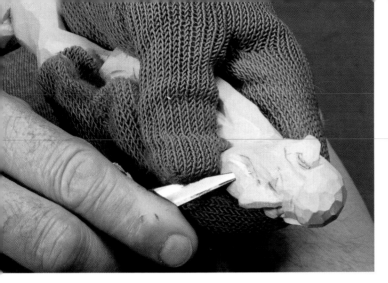

From the lip, trim off the ridges left by the gouge. This will thin the lip and bring out the cheeks.

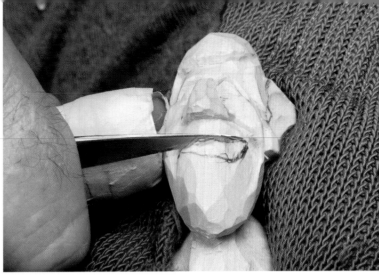

Work your way across the top lip cutting stops at a slightly obtuse angle into the mouth...

Progress.

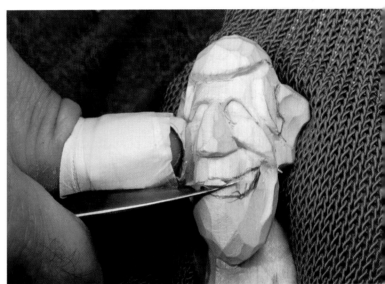

and trimming back to it from the mouth.

Time for another of Pete's rules. The art books tell you to put the mouth halfway between the bottom of the nose and the chin. On caricatures they look better closer to the nose. Draw the line of the inside of the mouth. Here's where the off-centered carving we did before can be appreciated.

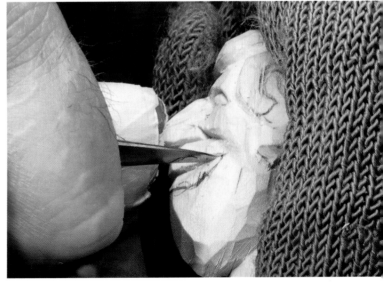

To make room for the teeth we need to take a wedge out of each corner. Make a deeper stop cut on the line of the top lip...

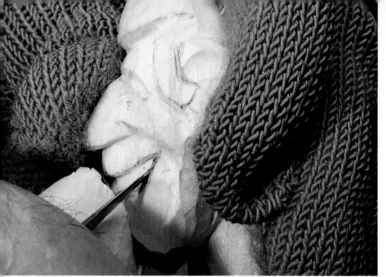

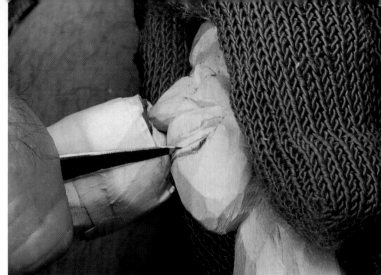

and on the bottom lip line.

Gradually make a stop cut in the tooth line. This is cross grain, so I may go over it six or seven times, using light cuts. If you try to apply too much pressure, the knife will crush the wood. When you start to cut the teeth they will be brittle and fall out.

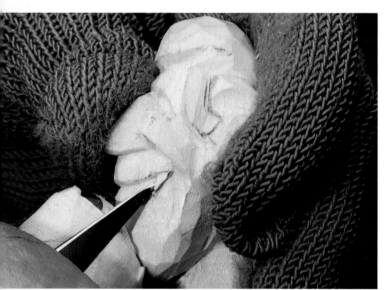

Pop the corner wedge out.

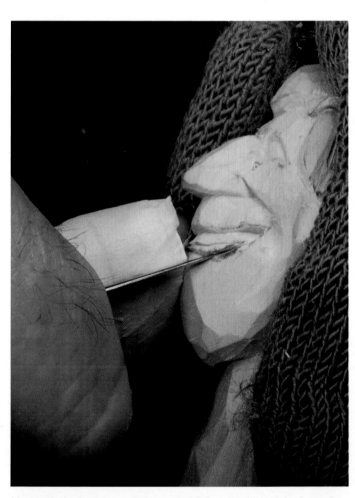

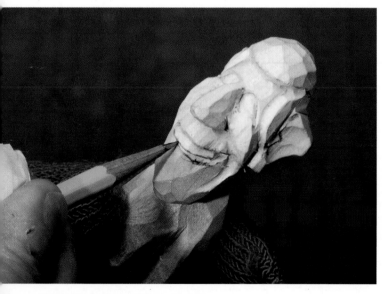

Draw the bottom of the top teeth.

Now with the knife at a slight angle I follow the line of the lower lip and cut a wedge back to the tooth line. Again this will take several lighter cuts to do it right.

Progress.

The result.

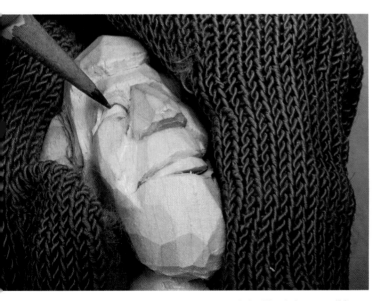

Start at the nose and draw the upper eyelids. The left one will be "squintier" than this one.

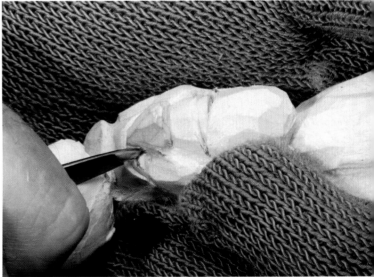

To carve eyes and teeth you need a fine-tipped knife. Gently cut a stop line into the eyelid line, starting at the nose. This, again, is a cross grain cut and you will need to make several passes.

43

Deepen the lower lid at the corners.

With the knife flat against the eyeball, pop out the corner between the lids. This will give curvature to the eyeball. Do this on both the inside and outside corners on both eyes.

The result.

Finally, shape the upper middle of the eyeball so the eyelid protrudes beyond it.

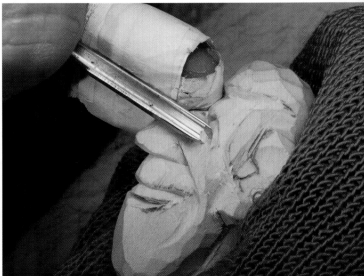

Use a small gouge to carve the bags under the eyes. I work from the center out...

44

and from the center in

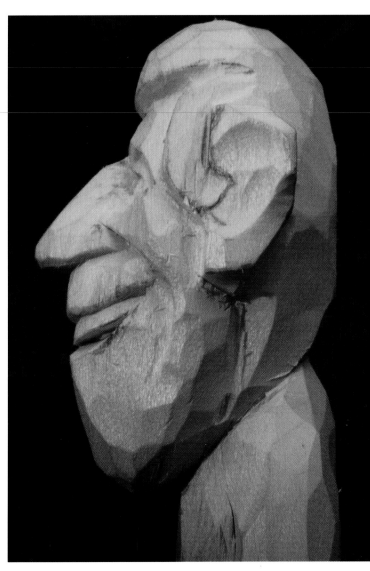

A side view reveals that the chin is protruding unnaturally forward. This is because when we smile or open our mouths, the jaw pivots and the chins moves back.

Progress.

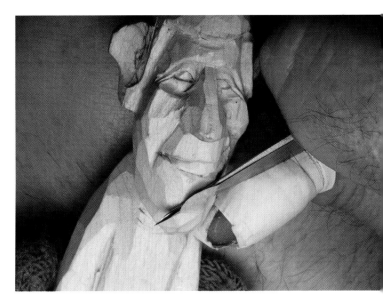

Though this is a tough step for some carvers to take, I next shave off the front of the chin to give it the proper angle. I start with a cut down the middle...

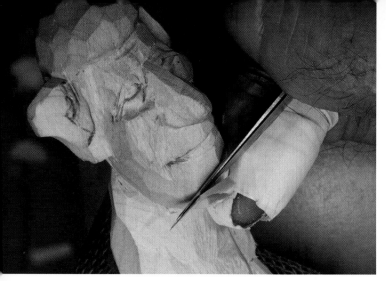

then one to this side...

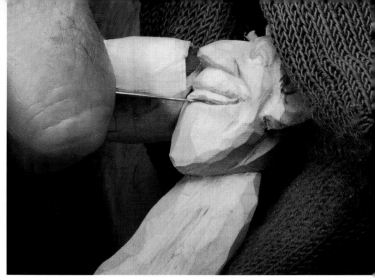

Slightly bevel the lower lip.

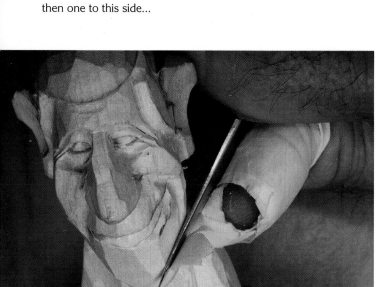

and that.

I like a few large teeth. I start at the center and cut a line.

The result is a much more natural line.

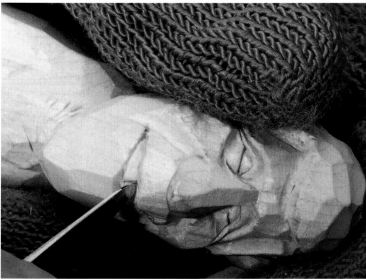

Then I make a small stop cut under the upper lip, on the top inside edge of both front teeth.

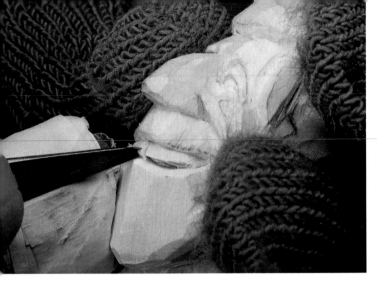

Thus allows me to pop out a wedge by cutting back to the center line from each tooth.

The method of carving the teeth is similar except that the wedge is only cut on the tooth to the back. This steps the teeth as they go back. Cut a stop in the gap, and one under the lip over the back tooth.

The result. Draw in the other teeth.

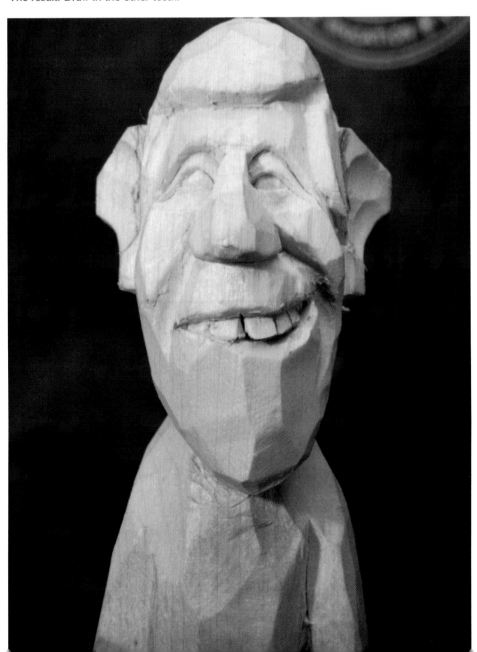

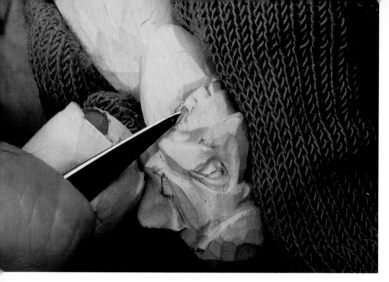

Cut a wedge from the forward edge of the back tooth only.

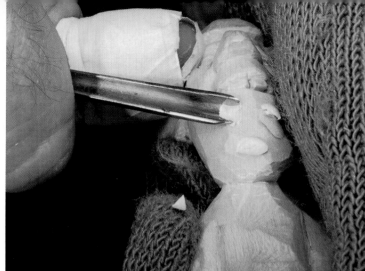

Use the same gouge and cut from the corners to the center under the lower lip.

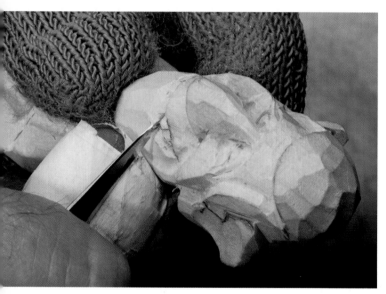

On the second and third teeth I cut a wedge from the bottom to give them a different length. This saves all the teeth from being unnaturally uniform.

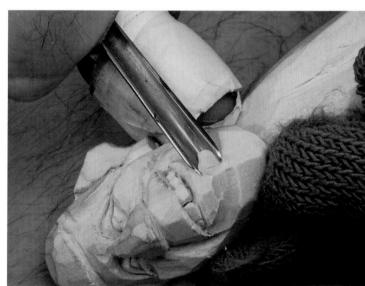

On the left side I'll exaggerate the cut to add some character.

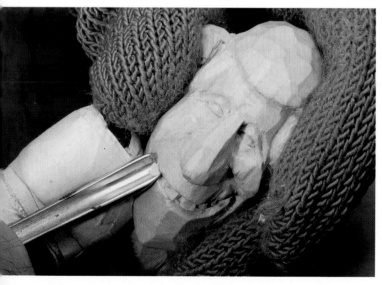

With a #9 gouge, come up across the outside corners of the lower lip, to make appear to be shorter than the upper lip.

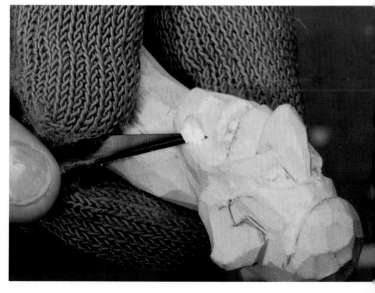

Blend in the gouge ridges with a knife.

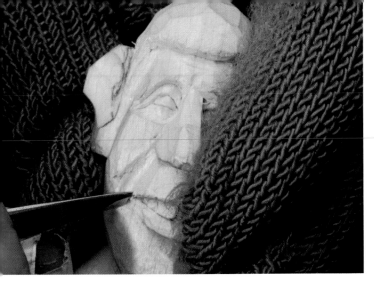

Make a stab cut right at the end of the mouth angled slightly back. This goes from the top lip to the lower lip.

Now I take a wedge out of the expression line to create a shadow. First cut an arching stop...

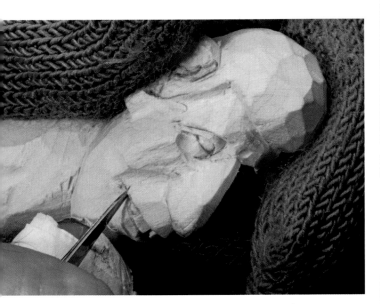

Cut down from the upper lip...

then cut back to it from the lip. Do the same on the other side.

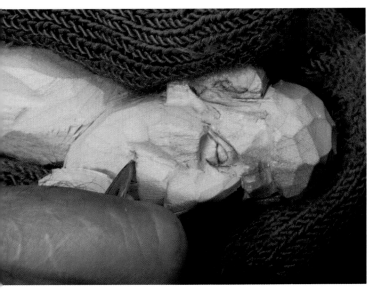

then pop out the triangular wedge. This will create a nice shadow, which is so important in caricature carving.

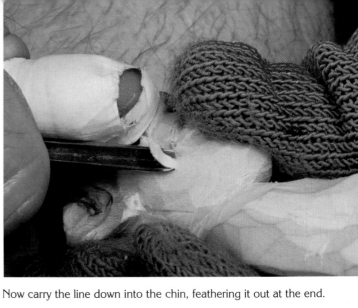

Now carry the line down into the chin, feathering it out at the end.

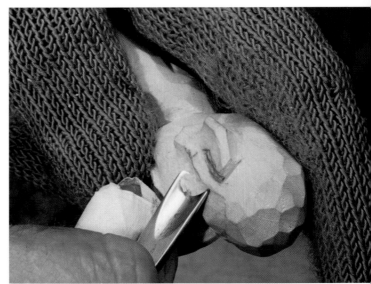

Progress. There is still too much wood in the cheeks and more flat surfaces than I like.

Two gouge cuts on each side give more character. First, on the right side cut back at the temple, going slightly down.

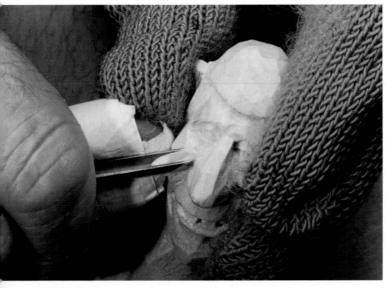

On top of the cheek, follow the expression line up to the eye, getting as close as you can to it.

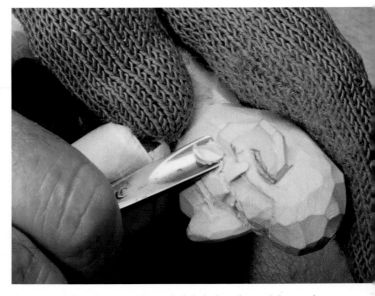

Second, at the expression line, slightly below the earlobe, make a second gouge cut up toward the earlobe.

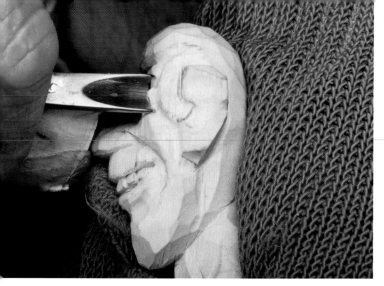

On the exaggerated left side the temple gouge cut goes straight back to the sideburn.

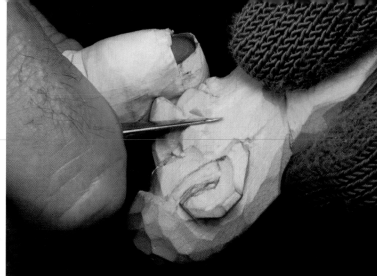

Blend the gouge ridges in to get rid of sharp angles.

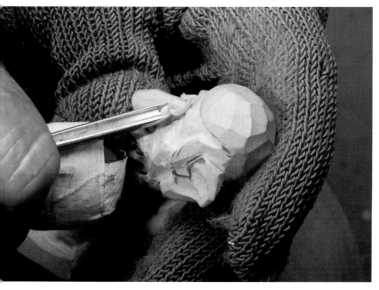

For the second cut I switch to a number 11 gouge and follow the expression line back to the eye.

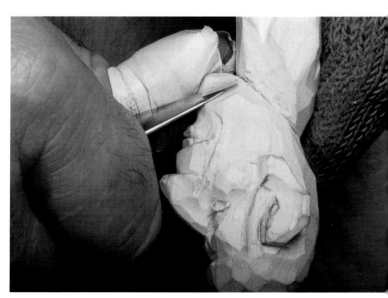

Make a scooping cut on both sides of the chin, making the left side more exaggerated. Blend the cuts into the face.

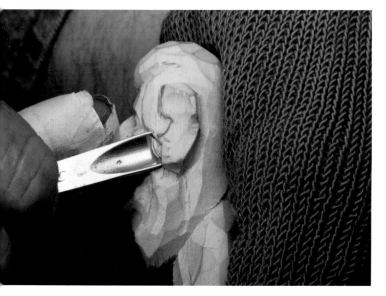

Using the wide gouge again, go back to the ear a little higher than on the right side. This will account for the smile.

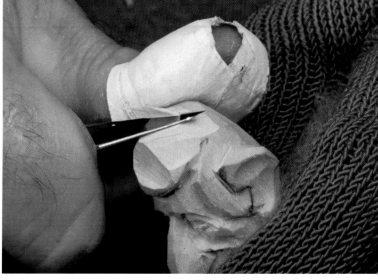

To begin the hair, I rough up the surface, making it less uniform. This gives the hair many more interesting planes.

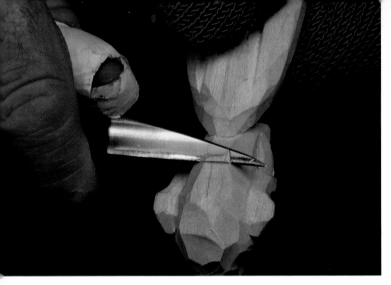

Make a stop cut in the back of the hairline and trim back to it from the neck.

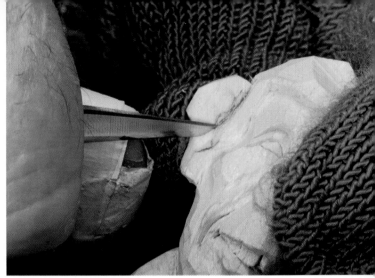

Follow the back edge of the sideburn into the ear with a stop cut.

In the same way carry the line over to the ears.

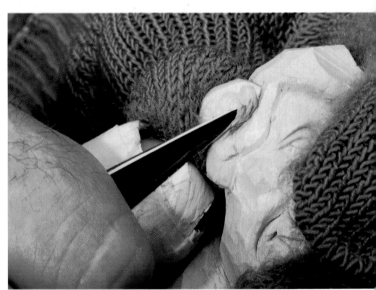

Cut back to it from the surface of the ear to make the ear look as though it comes behind the sideburn.

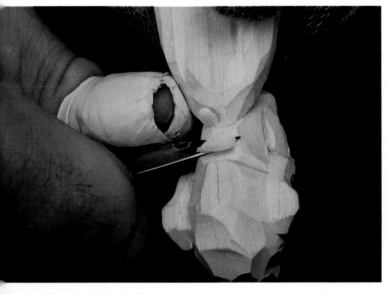

Shape the back of the neck.

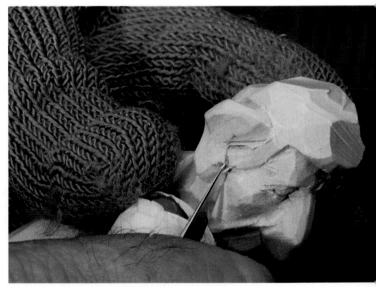

Do the same thing at the bottom of the sideburn.

The result.

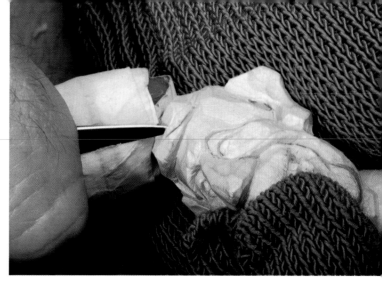

Cut back along the stop and pop out a wedge.

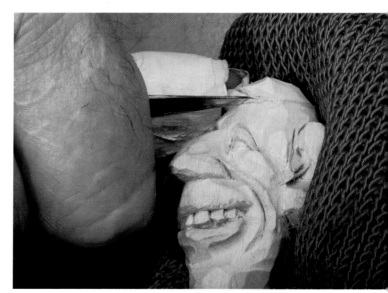

Cut a second line under the first, following the hairline in a wave.

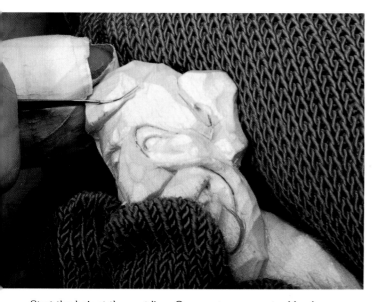

Start the hair at the part line. Carry a stop across and back.

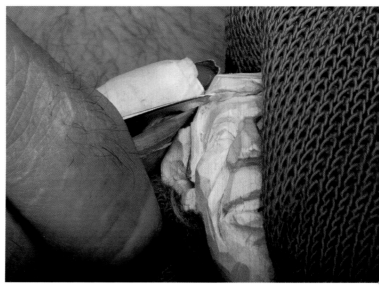

Yet a third time, cut another line, under the second, which comes up and over.

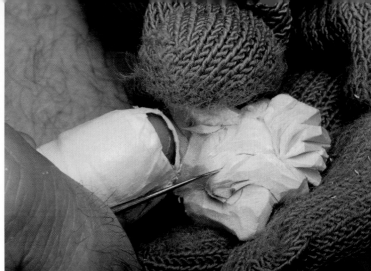

This gives the appearance of hair growing under the previous cut and being combed back over it.

A second cut starts under the first and curves up over it.

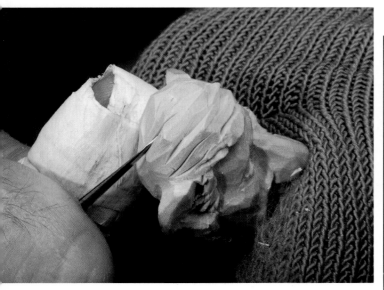

After the intricate front work, I cut a few major tresses combed back over the top of the head.

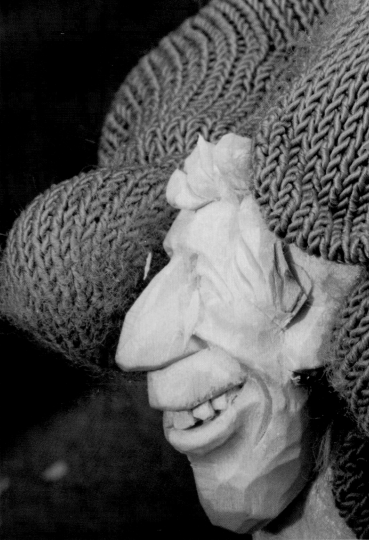

The result.

The sideburns are done the same way. A major cut starts at the part and flows down and back.

I go over flat areas between the major locks with a gouge to give them dimensionality.

With a #9 gouge deepen the ear at the ear canal.

I give texture to the ear by follow the outside shape with a gouge inside.

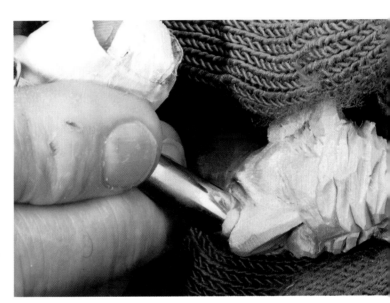

Create the nostril by coming in from the side with a gouge. Repeat on both sides.

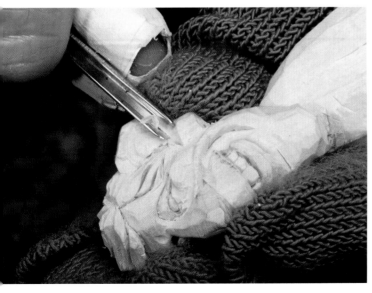

Do the same at the bottom, but cut in at the earlobe.

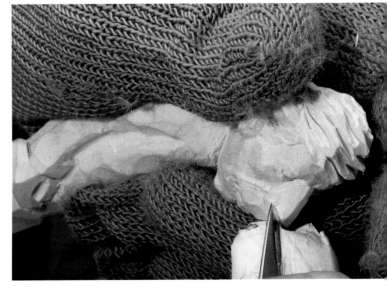

Cut a stop over the nostril...

55

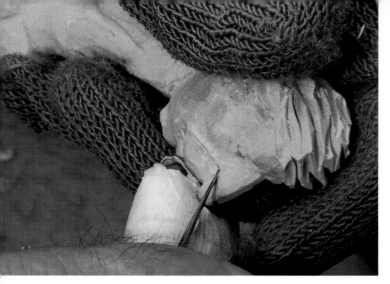

and back down over the nose to create the wing of the nose.

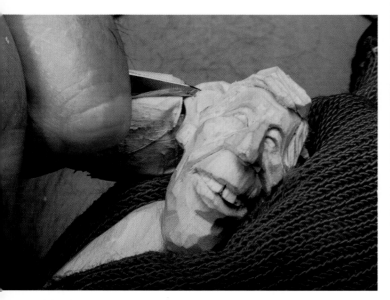

The final detail in the ear is a ridge created with the knife. Cut a stop...

The result.

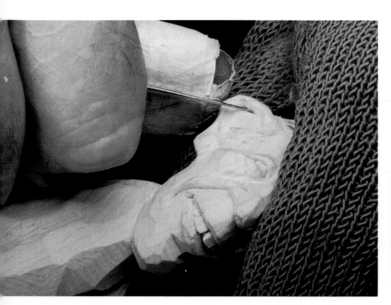

and come back to it from the center of the ear.

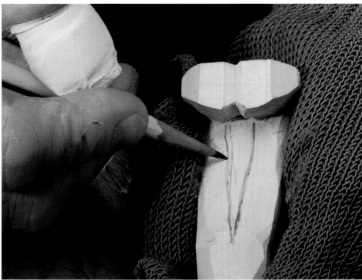

Moving back to the body, I want to open up this area between the lower legs.

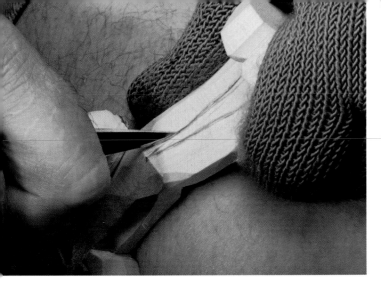

Cut a wedge by working one side...

After you get the opening, knock the corners off the legs before shaping them up.

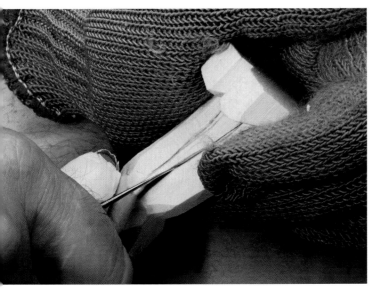

then the other.

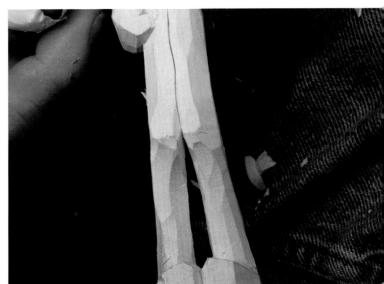

The result.

It takes a while, but finally, when the blade breaks through, you can work from both front and back and it gets much easier.

I like to get a little movement in the separation of the top of the legs, so the line I use isn't quite straight. Make a center cut...

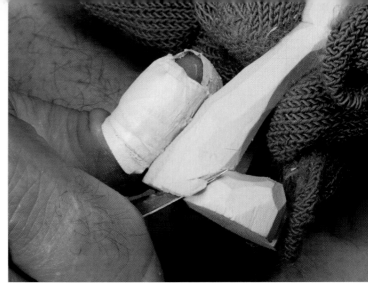

and come back to it from both sides to create the separation. Do the same on the back.

Cut back to the stop from the surface of the shoe.

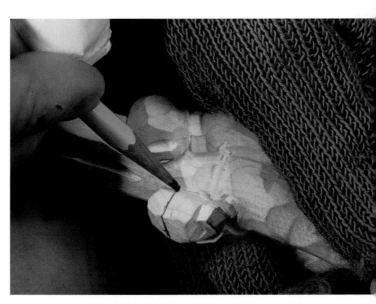

Round off the tops of the shoes, getting rid of any sharp edges.

Move to the hands and draw in the center line from the first knuckle to the finger tip. Do the same on the other hand.

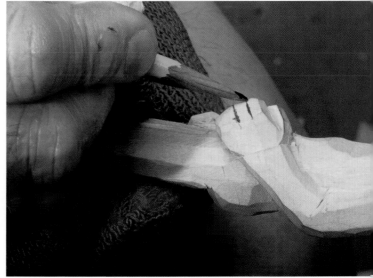

Make a stop cut for the cuff, from the heel to the top of the shoe.

Split the difference between the first two fingers.

The split between the other two is not quite equal because the ring finger is bigger than the pinky.

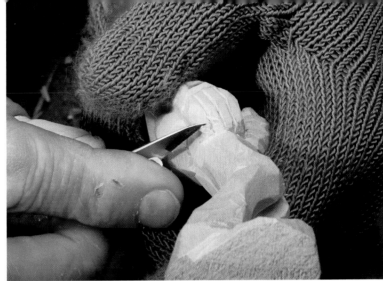

Round over the fingers, first evening the edges, then blending the surfaces.

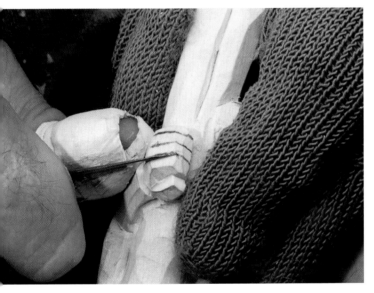

Make V-cuts on the lines to separate the fingers.

Outline the inside of the fingers with a stop cut.

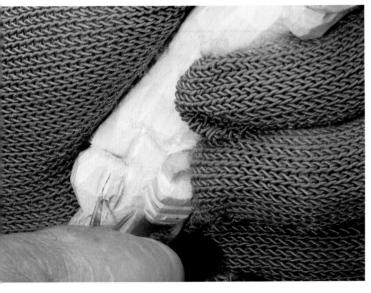

Highlight the thumb with the knife.

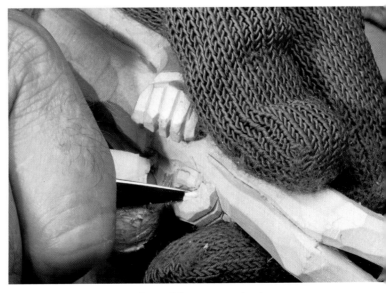

Then undercut the area in the middle to create depth.

The result.

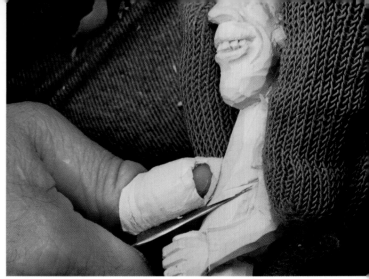

Cut some wedges out of the body to give it some interest. This is much more pleasing than a flat, featureless surface.

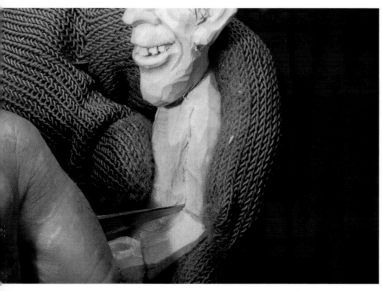

Create a line between the body and the arm. Like the legs, this should not be a straight line. Cut a stop.

Cut back to it to create depth, but don't do the same cut along the whole line. Vary it to create some contour.

Progress.

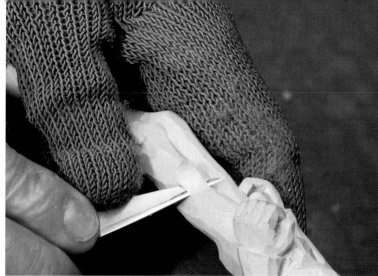

Do the same to the pants. I start at the top of the shoe and carry the line around the side. As I do so I break the side plane of the figure, which allows the viewer to see the wrinkle from the front and the side.

Scooping cuts add contour to the rest of the pants.

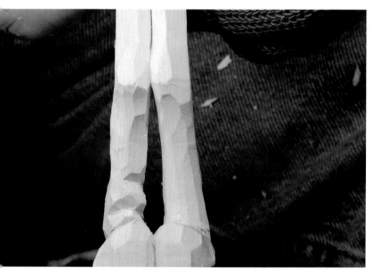

A couple more cuts and the leg begins to get really interesting.

Draw in a sole...

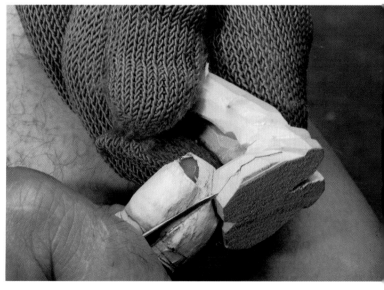

Cut wrinkles behind the knees.

and cut it with the knife. First make a stop cut...

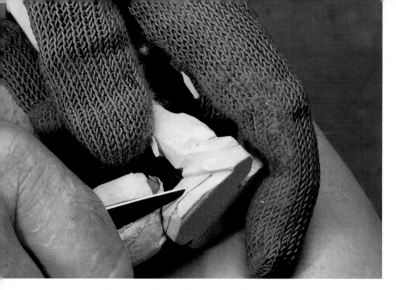

then come back to it from the upper side.

Progress.

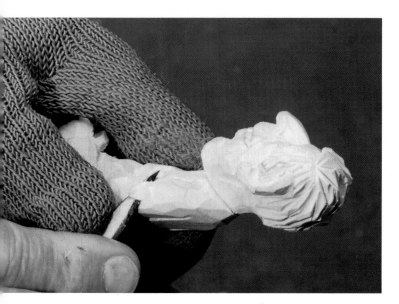

Cut into the arms at the elbows like you did with the legs.

Do the same thing on the back.

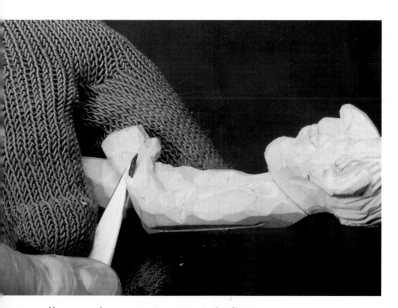

Use some long scooping cuts on the forearm.

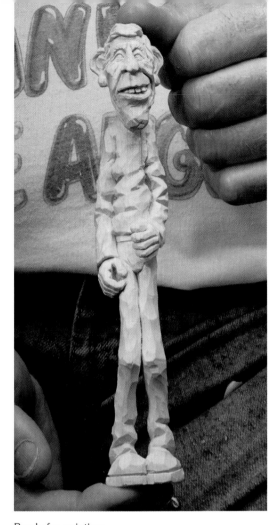

Ready for painting.

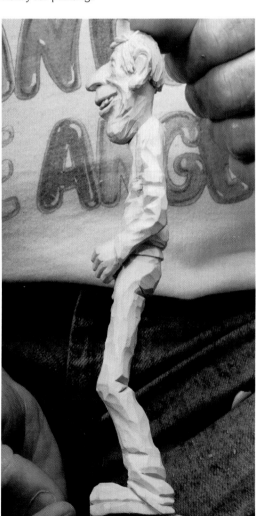

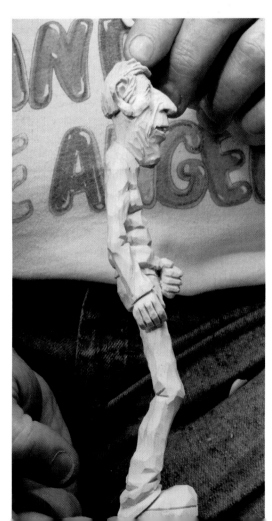

Painting

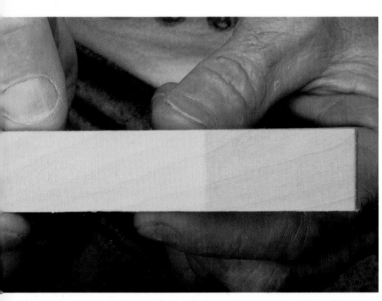

My base coat is boiled linseed oil and raw sienna, mixed to give me the yellowish color of Eastern Pine. I test it on a piece of scrap carved to remove planer or saw marks. I dip the wood in the base solution and let it set for a few minutes. This is the resultant color on the test piece.

Use the same wash for the teeth. Make sure you paint underneath the teeth to seal the mouth.

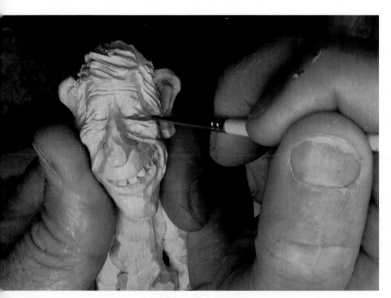

Turning to the actual piece, I do a little painting before I apply the base coat. I paint the eyeball with an off-white acrylic wash, using hobbyists acrylic colors. When this dries it creates a seal that the oil base coat will not penetrate

Add a dot of black paint for the pupil. This is a difficult thing to do. I get one eye the way I want it...

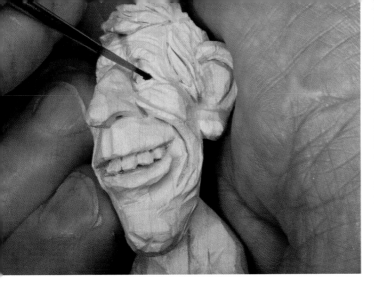

then paint the other.

Apply the base coat. While I am using a wide brush here, sometimes I dip the whole piece in a jar of the base coat.

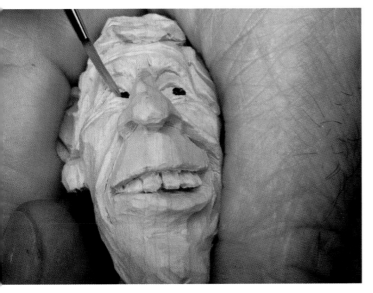

I use a light blue to outline the pupil of the eye with the iris.

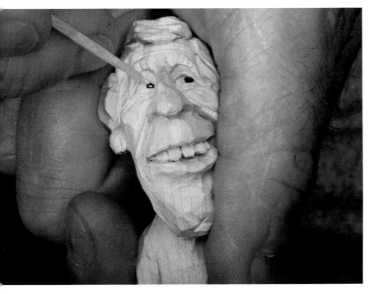

Use a toothpick to add a dot of white paint right out of the tube on each eye. Put it in the same position for each eye. This is the last step of acrylic painting before I apply the linseed oil/raw sienna base coat.

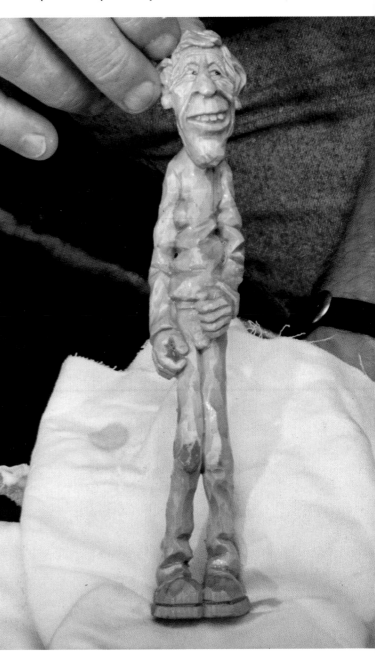

The base coat applied.

65

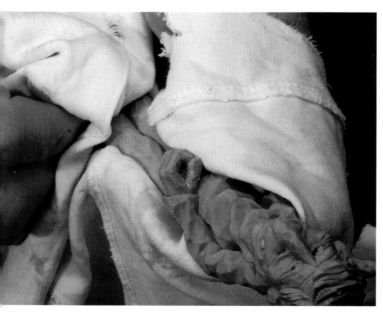

Wipe off the excess. I blow into the deeper areas to spread the oil out so I can wipe it away.

The flesh applied to the face.

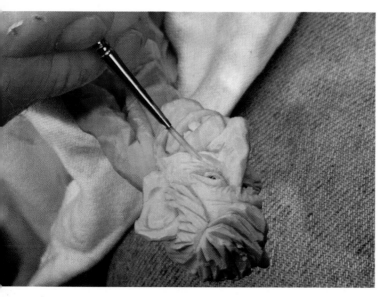

For the skin tones I use a medium flesh acrylic wash with a little cadmium red added to create a pinkish tone. Laying this over the yellowish undercoat gives a nice color. Apply this to all exposed skin surfaces. Because the oil is protecting the eyes, it doesn't matter if you paint right over them.

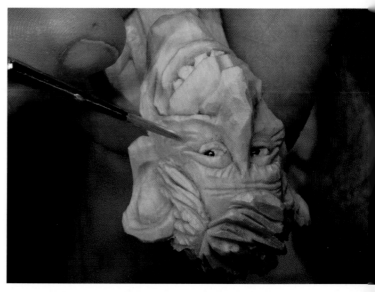

I add a light touch of cadmium red to the cheek bone...

the top of the ear...

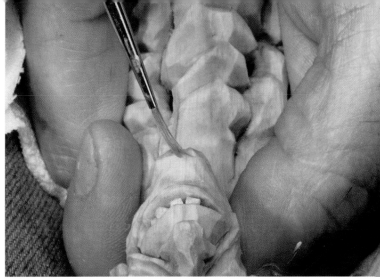

and the chin.

the ear lobe...

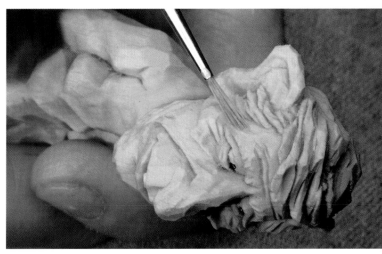

Sometimes I also use it on the temples, especially if the grain of the temple hasn't taken the base coat.

The face complete.

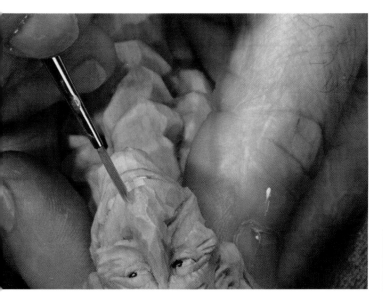

the tip of the nose...

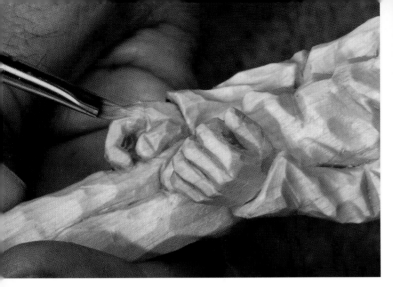

Add the flesh tones to the hands.

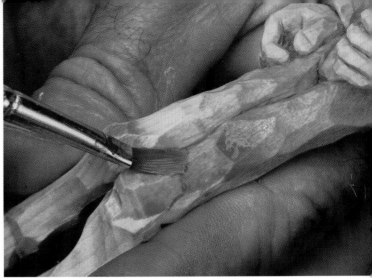

For the pants I am using a rust colored acrylic wash. Obviously you can choose any color you wish.

Add a little red highlight to the knuckles.

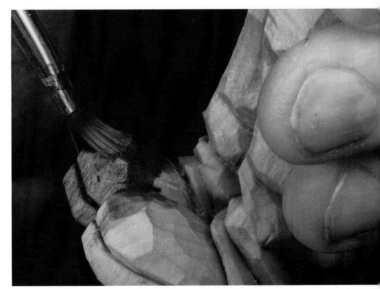

The shoes have a black wash.

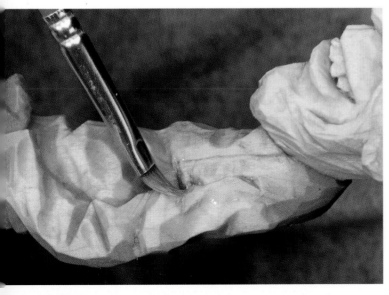

With the hands up against the body, I try to avoid reds for the clothing. I will choose a blue acrylic wash for the shirt.

Moving back to the head I will use a burnt umber wash for the hair. Around the face and eyebrows be careful. As you move back on the scalp things will move faster.

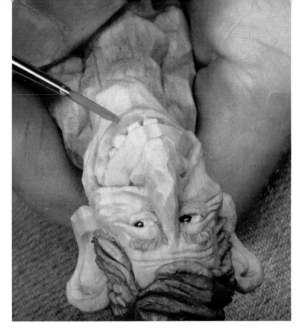

Add some color to the lower lip using a mixture of burnt sienna and a little cadmium red in a wash. I don't bother with the upper lip.

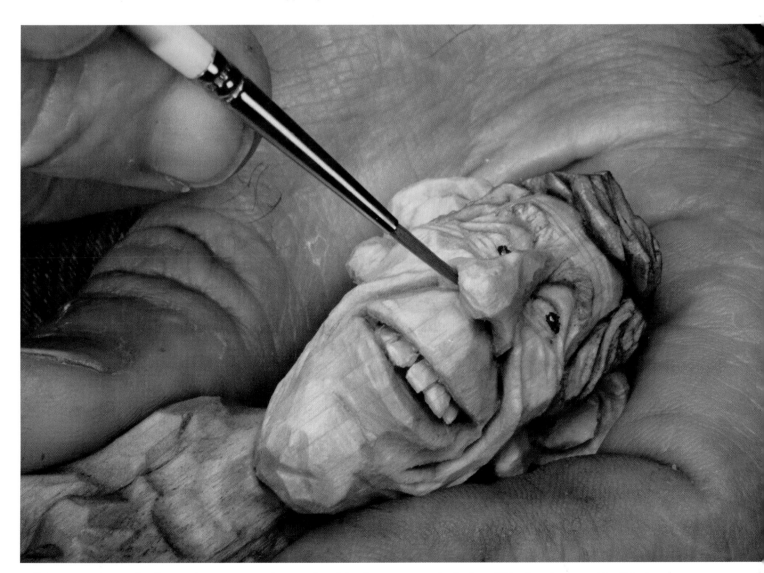

Using a very thin wash of burnt sienna, go over the nostril and the deeper creases in the face. This gives depth, making it looker deeper than it really is.

Gallery

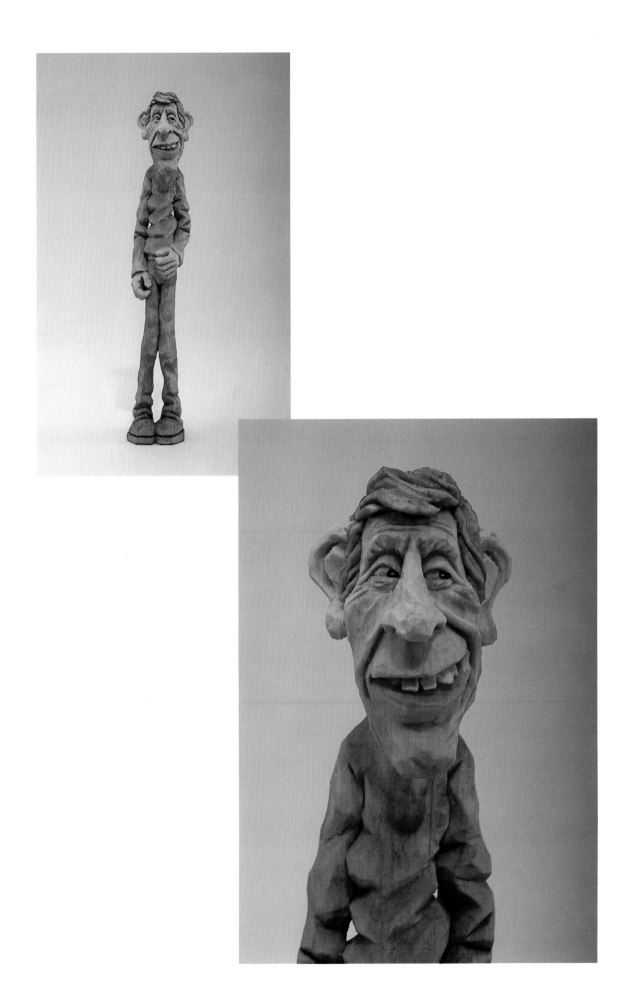

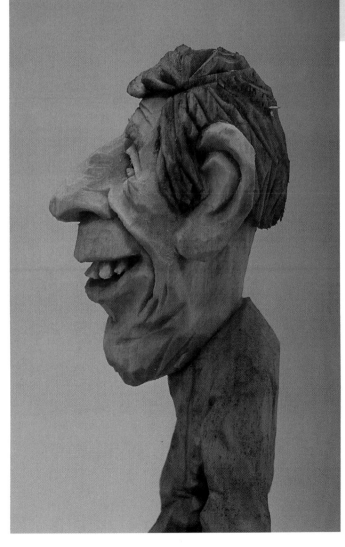

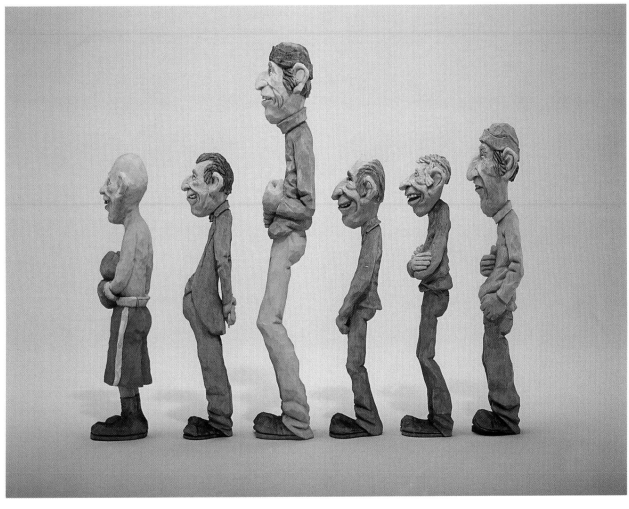

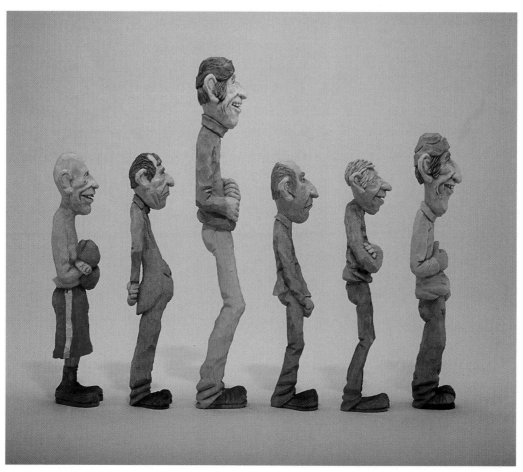

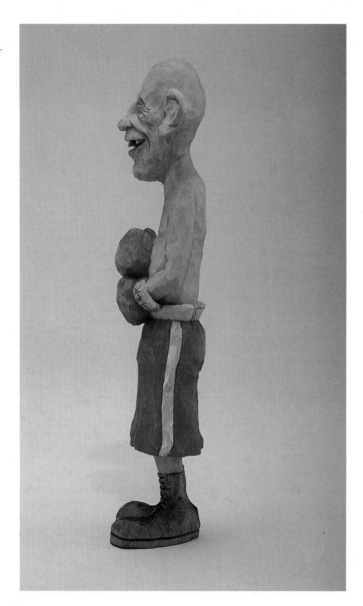